When Your Twenties Are Darker Than You Expected

By Paul C. Maxwell

Endorsements

"I'm so glad you're holding this book — *When Your Twenties Are Darker Than You Expected*. Paul's writing is like Tim Ferris meets Søren Kierkegaard — the tactical colliding with the existential. The tactical by itself will leave us numb. The existential alone will leave us in despair. If we need any tools to survive our twenties, it's this trail intersection, where we find Paul, where we find ourselves, and where we find our need for this writing."

— **Stephen Christian**, lead singer of Anberlin, and Worship Director at Calvary Alvuquerque.

"Paul Maxwell is the Kierkegaard of our generation. Christianity largely seems blind to the existential suffering of ambiguous adulthood. This is where this book shines. I hope it inspires a new genre of literature. Where every instinct is to critique feelings or to abandon theology, Paul interweaves them into a single metaphor. If you know what I mean when I say "Darkness," then you simply must buy this book. And if you are a parent of a twentysomething, then you need to buy two."

— **Daniel Montgomery**, Founder of Sojourn Network. Author, *Leadership Mosaic*.

"There are many reasons to ignore the negativity in our hearts. Most basically, it is intrinsically unpleasant, and when extreme, it is painful and usually gets us into trouble. So humans instinctively do their best to keep it out of awareness, and Christians often use the Bible to reinforce that instinct. Yet, the Law and the prophets, the Psalms and Job, culminating with the life and death of Jesus would actually seem to promote greater awareness of the negativity in our hearts, so that God's word and Word might saturate more and more of our life, inner and outer.

This book, then, is exemplary, as well as unique: raw, confessional, and devotional; something like Augustine meets Sylvia Plath; a witness of darkness greater than *The Confessions*, but similarly infused with truth and grace. Perhaps it portends a new genre of Christian literature. I hope so. Sure, it's a minority report; not everyone has had this much inner turmoil. But such transparency is a gift to the whole church, for it helps those with great darkness come to terms with it in Christ and helps those with less darkness understand those with more.

— **Eric Johnson**, Lawrence and Charlotte Hoover Professor of Pastoral Care, Southern Baptist Theological Seminary. Author, *Foundations of Soul Care: A Christian Psychology Proposal*, and *God and Soul Care: The Therapeutic Resources of the Christian Faith*.

"Paul Maxwell is one of the brightest minds and deepest thinkers I know. More than that, his passion for the gospel and its ability to work in us even in our darkest moments is infectious. I'm happy to commend this unique, insightful, and poignant book to you—a book I wish I'd read in my twenties."

— Brandon D. Smith, author of *Rooted: Theology for Growing Christians.*

"Your twenties aren't always dark, but struggling with issues like anxiety, discontentment, and depression are not outlier experiences. All too often, though, our advice in the Church falls into broad platitudes or "Jesus-jukes" that don't deal with the disorienting and painful realties of the twenty-somethings in our pews. In *When Your Twenties Are Darker Than You Expected*, Paul Maxwell manages to avoid the common clichés all the while pointing us to the Jesus real enough to meet us in our darkness. All I can say is that I wish someone had given me this book when I was doing college and young adult ministry. I highly recommend this if you're a twenty-something, or the parent or pastor of one.

— Derek Rishmawy, is a systematic theology PhD student at Trinity Evangelical Divinity School. He contributes to *Christ and Pop Culture*, *Christianity Today*, and writes at his own blog, *Reformedish*. He also co-hosts a podcast called *Mere Fidelity*. You can follow him on Twitter at @DZRishmawy.

When Your Twenties are Darker than You Expected is helpful in so many ways. First of all, each chapter is an invitation to honesty. As a counselor I've come to learn that putting your experience in your own words is a step that cannot be skipped. The psalmist exhorts us to "pour out your hearts to him" (Psalm 62:8) so the more ways you have of understanding and articulating your experience the better. Paul poignantly describes the many ways he's found his twenties to be difficult. His writing is studded with thoughtful allusions, poetic phrases, and images. Mine them for their riches. Meditate on them. Let them stimulate you to add your words to his in conversation with God and others.

— Winston Smith, CCEF Faculty and Counselor, and Priest in Charge at Saint Anne's Episcopal Church, Abington, PA.

Dedication

Mom, you are the strongest,
most beautiful, most loving
person I know.

You deserve so much to be loved.
If I ever accomplish anything in life,
I hope it is to love you well — to love you
 better than I have, so far.

It has been my single greatest privilege these 29 years
— through my constant, unforgivable selfishness —
to be your beloved son.

If I have anyone to thank for
these trinkets; these gifts —
my EQ and IQ —
it is you.

May I never make the mistake
of valuing them
more than you.

Barbara Lynn Marrine,
this book is a tribute to your
ten thousand days of never
giving up on me.

And, it is dedicated to you.

Table of Contents

Foreword
By Stephen Christian of Anberlin

My twenties were the worst years of my life for one reason alone:

I believed that everyone had life figured out *except for me.*

I felt like all my friends in their twenties were finally having their teenage fantasies of adulthood finally coming true.

My lowest point was at 22 years old. I had graduated with my Associates of Arts — a 2 year degree. I moved to Tampa, FL and slept on my friend's couch for 8 months while I operated the Kumba roller coaster at Busch Gardens theme park. I was so lulled into daily life that by the time I was 23, I had no place of my own. I was barely scraping by with my theme park paycheck. By that time, all my friends were married, and I felt so incapable. I felt lost. Life felt aimless — pointless.

Even though I was in a band, we didn't get signed until I was 25. In fact, until I turned 25, my life was pure hell. I would call those the "Aimless Years." Because of that time, I made some tragic decisions — like losing my virginity — because I felt so helpless and hopeless. I think it was those years that made me feel incapable — incompetent — and I carried that baggage into my relationships with me. By the time someone showed me a hint of love and care, all of my guards were crumbled on the floor. My self-esteem was so ravaged by my felt incompetence, standing sheepishly underneath my perception of everyone else succeeding and growing and "adult-ing," my sense of dignity was hollow, empty. So, in that time, losing my virginity felt like a second-nature mistake — I had sunken into a place of despair, mixed with numbing devices to distract me from that despair.

My twenties brought me to the point where I felt like my life was truly meaningless:

"I won't amount to anything."
"I don't have the life that everyone else has, and I never will."

It was almost like mental suicide. Growing up ADHD, my guidance counselor told me I was going to have a menial job. Then, when I went to college and felt completely inadequate, I just thought, "This is it! I'm just going to bounce around from crap job to crap job. Maybe my guidance counselor was right. I should have just been an auto mechanic."

Even signing a record deal had its own challenges. I didn't move out of my parents' house until I was 29. Besides my short stint in Tampa, all my years were with my parents. Yes, I was touring with a band, but I was borrowing money from my parents to pay my cell phone bill, because the all the money we made from Anberlin just went right back into it. It wasn't until our 3rd record that the band made any money. I looked at all my friends with 401ks and kids and marriage, and that translated into my deep feeling of incompetence.

For me, realizing the success of Anberlin made me finally feel confident. That finally kickstarted me out of my cycle, and propelled me into believing in myself.

If I had one piece of advice to give people hope in their twenties, it's this:

Time brings clarity.

Your perspective on life is clearer at age 15 than it is at age 5. And it gets clearer at 25 than 15. And clearer at 35 than 25. Maybe that's a lesson only time can teach. But, it's those years — between 20 and 25 — that you just feel so lost.

Just hold on to the hope that time will take care of that. All those feelings that seem impossible to process are completely normal. Even if you have a great job in your early 20s, you might still be asking yourself: "Should I be here?" And the answer might be "No!" The average person will switch jobs 6 times in their lifetime. Just don't take the constant, never-ending feeling of "being insufficient" or "being in transition" as a sign that it will last forever. It won't.

Every decade of our lives has its unique kind of hardship. Our twenties just happen to be our decade of sucky darkness that force us to either numb our pain, or develop strategies for emotional resilience.

I'm so glad you're holding this book — *When Your Twenties Are Darker Than You Expected*. Paul's writing is like Tim Ferris meets Søren Kierkegaard — the tactical colliding with the existential. The tactical by itself will leave us numb. The existential alone will leave us in despair. If we need any tools to survive our twenties, it's this trail intersection, where we find Paul, where we find ourselves, and where we find our need for this writing.

Foreword

By Winston Smith
Episcopal Priest

When Paul Maxwell first starting talking to me about his own life as a Millennial as a sort of "quarter-life crisis," it caught me off guard. I did that funny head-tilt dogs do when they hear an unfamiliar sound. But in about thirty seconds I knew he was onto something and I've been excited about this book ever since.

I'll admit, I've always resisted the modern need to label generations. As a "GenXer" I never liked the quasi-honorary status conferred on "Baby Boomers," and I resent having a label that essentially identifies me as one fated to live in their shadow. I suspect "Millennials" have equally sensible reasons for resenting their label. We naturally resist being herded into obscenely broad categories that don't recognize us as individuals who are more than the product of our moment in history and culture. We don't want to be hexed by our generational label any more than we want to be fated for being born under an astrological sign. (But maybe that's just a GenXer being cynical.)

On the other hand, while generational labels don't tell us much about the personal character of those who bear them, they do remind us of the unique circumstances that modern generations have faced. "The Greatest Generation" survived the Great Depression and fought and won World War II. The "Baby Boomers" saw the dawn of the Cold War and inaugurated the sexual revolution. "GenXers", well, we lived in the wake of all of that. Millennials have come of age in their own set of unprecedented circumstances. I think of it as an age of sociological tremors and shifting sand. It's a post 911 era of terror alerts, lone wolf attacks, and endless war in the Middle East. They've survived the Great Recession, witnessed the first African-American president, been sensitized to innumerable racial and social justice issues, and are navigating a complete re-visioning of what marriage, sexuality, and even gender mean.

As Paul's friend and a father of three Millenials myself, my humble observation is that one of the challenges that they face is that as young adults they live in a culture that confers upon them all of the challenges of adulthood while they are yet years away from the personal and social structures that normally undergird those challenges. For instance, most of them have been told that family and career don't really begin until after college. But for many, "college" means earning a master's or doctoral degree and that's just to get to the starting gate of their career. They live as adults waiting to get started, in a sense, waiting for life to begin. Meanwhile, they face all of the emotional pressures of early adulthood — a desire for lasting intimacy, independence, and the need for purpose and meaning, but without marriage, job, and family to support them. It's frustrating, disillusioning, even depressing.

Paul has been courageous enough to let us peek into his own experience of life as a twenty-something. Without either whining or pulling punches, he offers himself to us as a humble and wise fellow traveler. You may know Paul from his thoughtful blogging and posts on Desiring God. That should tell you enough, but I've had the privilege of knowing Paul as both a student and friend and I've come to know him as a reliable guide in understanding the spiritual journey and tasks of people in his generation. He is one of the most intelligent people I know, fiercely honest, and genuine. That's the kind of companion and guide you need.

When Your Twenties are Darker than You Expected is helpful in so many ways. First of all, each chapter is an invitation to honesty. As a counselor, I've come to learn that putting your experience in your own words is a step that cannot be skipped. The psalmist exhorts us to "pour out your hearts to him" (Psalm 62:8) so the more ways you have of understanding and articulating your experience the better. Paul poignantly describes the many ways he's found his twenties to be difficult. His writing is studded with thoughtful allusions, poetic phrases, and images. Mine them for their riches. Meditate on them. Let them stimulate you to add your words to his in conversation with God and others.

Perhaps most importantly, Paul explores biblical themes that suggest ways that God joins the conversation. As Paul says, he isn't into "life hacks" or "Jesus jukes" — just offering starting places to engage God and feel your way forward in what can be very dark moments. *When*

Your Twenties is not about easy answers, but a way for the conversation to get started. In sense, Paul isn't just letting us into his personal struggle but into a conversation with God that is well underway and hoping that you might join in.

This book is one of many ways that I see the wisdom that God is nurturing in the Millennial generation. As you read it I believe you will come to the same conclusion.

Introduction

> Back and forth across
> time, lots of things
> one needs one's
>
> hand held for. Don't
> stumble, in the dark. Keep
> walking. This is life.
> —Robert Creeley[1]

If I was writing this book 500 years ago, I would have called it, *Christianity for God's Odd Species of Christian, The Twenty-Something, Who Strives and Wanders, Who Gets Up Late and Goes to Bed Early (Without Going to Sleep), Who Both Loves Ecclesiastes and Quickly Forgets Why, Who is Neither Innocent Nor Wise, Who Is Bitter and Brave About Old-Life's New Disappointments, For Me, and Therefore For Others.*[2] I am not an expert on twentysomethings, which is to say that I am not a pretend sociologist. Literature for this audience is *saturated* with self-proclaimed "millennial experts."

---

[1] Robert Creeley, "You," *The Collected Poems of Robert Creeley: 1945-1975* (Los Angeles: University of California Press, 1962), 501.

[2] I also would not have had Spotify 500 years ago. Thank God we weren't alive then. If I may — would you read this book while listening to music? I listened to music while I wrote it. Nothing with words, of course. *The Revenant* soundtrack is unbeatab;e. The more reflective trance music like Oceanlab's "Clear Blue Water." Something meaningfully contemplative, and instrumental.

Gilbert Rouget tells us this about music: "when it is a success, music creates the feeling of total adhesion of the self to what is happening," Gilbert Rouget, *Music and Trance: A Theory of the Relations Between Music and Possession*, trans. Brunhilde Biebuyck (Chicago: The University of Chicago Press, 1985), 123. "What is happening" in this case is deep knowledge work in your most difficult of emotions. Music is an affective tool with which our troubled hearts cannot afford to dispense.

One blog on twentysomethings starts this way: "On a recent press tour for my new book in New York City, I spent time telling dozens of media outlets the story of what the millennial generation is going through." I have no desire to go to New York City, or to spend time with media outlets, or to explain to others what twentysomethings are going through. I'm a 27 year-old who lives on a college campus and still borrows money from his mom.

If this book would be truly helpful, it can't be *on* or *for* twentysomethings. It must be for me, and for us. It must face adult issues *as* adult issues, not as twentysomething issues. It must highlight the *crisis* of "Quarter-Life Crisis" — whether that is dissatisfaction, despair, depression, or the like.

Not every reader will find this book helpful. It may be *unhelpful*. Some will find it too secular, and others too Christian. I'm satisfied with that dilemma. But, before you read this book, I want you to understand what it is, and why it has its shape. In reading this brief introduction, I hope to give you a sense of perspective and mission — not on your twenties, but on your reading of this book. I hope that it isn't easy to read. It wasn't easy to write.

A Brief Note on the Footnotes

In one sense, this book is not for "twentysomthings" at all. It is for adults. And adults are uncoddled and unprotected. We are, as John

---

University of Chicago professor and composer Leonard Meyer insists: "Tensions arising from psychic needs may be worked off in sheer physical activity which is without meaningful relation to the original stimulus or to the tendency itself. In music, on the other hand, the same stimulus, the music, activates tendencies, inhibits them, and provides meaningful resolutions." Leonard B. Meyer, *Emotion and Meaning in Music* (Chicago: The University of Chicago Press, 1956), 23. Successful music, unlike "stress relieving" strategies such as exercise, supplies our anxiety experience with materially significant content, unspoken as it may be — music is content as much as words, and it is especially relevant content to the experience of reading about one's own anxiety, our present task. A brief, but fascinating (yet slightly technical) chapter on the relationship between music and the reading experience can be found here: P. N. Johnson-Laird and Keith Oatley, "Emotions, Music, and Literature," in Michael Lewis, Jeannette M. Haviland-Jones, and Lisa Feldman Barrett (eds.), *Handbook of Emotions*, 3rd ed. (New York: The Guilford Press, 2009), 102-113.

Paul Sartre might say, "condemned to be free."[3] And with that condemnation comes the blossoming beauty of increased responsibility. We bear the full consequences of our decisions. We should have been taught better. We should have been imbued with more skill. But here we are, uninformed and unskilled, in a world in which we are responsible for all our actions and emotions. That is a scary thing.

The condemnation to be free compels some of us to be *autodidacts* — the "self-taught," rather than the learned.[4] Publishing went through a transition in the 1990's in which good writing was equated with a lack of footnote: "Annotation was out; breezy, uninterrupted prose was in."[5]

This transition inaugurated a genre of literature adopted largely by mainstream Christian publishing houses.[6] But footnotes are for those in desperate need.[7] The suicidal. The depressed. The failing. The despairing. I am a member of these groups.

I will speak for myself, and perhaps for some others: in moments when an emotion has caught me by the neck, I want to know what it is. I want to understand myself, to see where others have been, what others have said, what skillful warriors and victors and failures have felt and done.[8]

Footnotes are a place to meet those people. For those who want information that goes as deeply as their emotions, I have provided them. For those who cannot stand footnotes, the main text of the book is not

---

[3] John Paul Sartre, *Being and Nothingness: A Phenomenological Essay on Ontology*, trans. Hazel E. Barnes (New York: Washington Square Press, 1992; originally Gallimard, 1943), 567.

[4] As John Piper insists about intellectual inquiry: "It's not about going to school or getting degrees or having prestige. It's not about the superiority of intellectuals. It's about using the means God has given us to know him, love him, and serve people." John Piper, *Think: The Life of the Mind and the Love of God* (Wheaton, IL: Crossway, 2011), 17.

[5] Jenny Lyn Bader, "Forget Footnotes. Hyperlink," *The New York Times*, July 16, 2000. http://partners.nytimes.com/library/review/071600footnotes-review.html. Accessed on July 30, 2016.

[6] "Footnotes distress publishers, who unfortunately lurk behind every book. They find notes unsightly, costly, forbidding." Chuck Zerby, *The Devil's Details: A History of Footnotes* (New York: Touchstone, 2002), 2.

[7] It would be an error to say that the footnote is an academic contrivance. "One of the earliest and most ingenious inventions of humankind, the footnote has been for centuries an indispensible tool of the scholar and a source of endlessly varied delight for the layperson." Zerby, *The Devil's Details*, 1.

[8] "To the inexpert, footnotes look like deep root systems, solid and fixed; to the connoisseur, however, they reveal themselves as anthills, swarming with constructive and combative activity." Anthony Grafton, *The Footnote: A Curious History* (Cambridge, MA: Harvard University Press, 1997), 9.

dependent upon them, so feel free to skip them entirely.

A Brief Note on Trauma

"Trauma" is quickly becoming the 21st century term for "suffering" — it has become our grownup word for "ouch," despite the clinically stringent guidelines of its use in academic psychology. Having the word "trauma" in our tool belt is necessary, because it is an important element of our emotional literacy (more below). But thinking of ourselves as traumatized people (i.e., victims) can sometimes undermine the very resiliency we need to overcome the trauma.[9] It's almost as if knowing pain *with* the word "trauma" ties us to all the baggage that comes along with it in more extreme settings, and we get bogged down in all of these symptoms of trauma that we think we're supposed to have when our healing process doesn't require the word.

We both need and overuse the word. Therefore, I hope that my next book will be totally on trauma. However, this book *ought* to have a chapter on the concept — I think it is probably the unifying theme of every chapter. But I'm finding that I simply haven't understood the concept deeply enough yet to write well about it in only a few thousand words. I hope you'll forgive me for not treating it at length here.[10]

---

[9] See Nick Haslam, "Concept Creep: Psychology's Expanding Concepts of Harm and Pathology," *Psychological Inquiry* 27, no. 1 (2016): 1-17. See a piece in The Atlantic disussing the article here:
https://www.theatlantic.com/politics/archive/2016/04/concept-creep/477939/.

[10] I initially recommend this smattering of books: Judith L. Herman, *Trauma and Recovery: The Aftermath of Violence—From Domestic Abuse to Political Terror* (New York: Basic Books, 1992); Bessel van der Kolk, *The Body Keeps Score: Brain, Mind, and Body in the Healing of Trauma* (New York: Penguin, 2014); Peter A. Levine and Bessel van der Kolk, *Trauma and Memory: Brain and Body in a Search for the Living Past: A Practical Guide for Understanding and Working with Traumatic Memory* (Berkeley, CA: North Atlantic Books, 2015); Peter A. Levine, *In an Unspoken Voice: How the Body Releases Trauma and Restores Goodness* (Berkeley, CA: North Atlantic Books, 2010); Peter A. Levine, *Waking the Tiger: Healing Trauma* (Berkeley, CA: North Atlantic Books, 1997); Richard Gartner, *Beyond Betrayal: Taking Charge of Your Life after Boyhood Sexual Abuse* (Hoboken, NJ: John Wiley & Sons, 2005); David Emerson and Elizabeth Hopper, *Overcoming Trauma through Yoga: Reclaiming Your Body* (Berkeley, CA: North Atlantic Books, 2011).

The "Two Voices" in Every Chapter

In 1908, a doctor named Kurt Koldstein reported a case of a woman with an odd disorder — she had no control over one of her hands. Her hand would rip off her bed sheets, spill her drinks on her, and even try to choke her. This was the first reported case of what was later called "alien-hand syndrome," and by some, "the Dr. Strangelove effect."[11] It is, as you might guess, caused by the damaging of nerve fibers in the brain. But we all have something similar.

We enter our twenties with the expectations of harmony that was offered us as a child, and all of a sudden, life and the universe slap us with such discord that we suffer from cognitive dissonance — that our souls are composed of two voices; an "alien-desire syndrome." Some voices drag us down to the pits of emotional hell. Others strengthen us, even rescue us.

One of the reasons our twenties can be so emotionally confusing is because we don't know how to distinguish between those two voices. We simply believe every voice we hear in our head — it would be as if the woman with the uncontrollable hand believed every intention of her out-of-control hand to be indicative of her true intention, as if she *wanted* to be dragged out of bed, and covered in her drink, and choked to death. But she didn't. And she knew we didn't. And each chapter in this book gives voice to both the negative and the positive voices in order that we might distinguish them, and juxtapose them, and find God's true intention for us in the midst of our alien-desires. These desires *are us*, and in many ways represent legitimate concerns to which we must listen.

Emotional Literacy

One of the most important skills that our twenties requires us to cultivate is the ability to understand what our emotions are telling us — that's what the "two voices" attempt to do, to verbalize the difficult

---

[11] Daniel B. Smith, *Muses, Madmen, and Prophets: Rethinking the History, Science, and Meaning of Auditory Hallucination* (New York: Penguin, 2007), 33-46.

language of emotions into words we can understand. We must learn, not just to analyze and deduct what certain emotions *say about us*, but rather shift our thinking to "read" our emotions so that we can hear what they are *saying to us*.

We humans communicate to each other with signs — words, raised eyebrows, head nods, hand gestures, even silence itself. We use these symbols to represent an idea that we want to share with someone else: a meal, a feeling, an offense, a command. Our emotions must be conceived the same way: as *signs* to us, representing realities about ourselves which must be heard. They are not infallible, and they are certainly not always accurate.

But our emotions work *for us* better (rather than *against us*) when we stop trying to dissect them in order to reject and demean them, and start listening to them, in order to hear the truth about what is happening in our minds, bodies, hearts, and souls.[12]

Emotions, like words in a book, have meaning embedded in them. In each of the emotions we explore in this book, the task is to tease out — to "translate" — our emotional symbols into verbal sentences. The quickening heartbeat, the rapid Alice-tumbling-down-the-rabbit-hole fears and hatred that twist our delicate bodies into knots before our very eyes — this cluster of experiences can be translated as: "I'm scared, because I'm vulnerable, and I don't want to be humiliated."

When we learn to see our emotions as "signs" with meaning pointing to something else — as the language that our bodies and souls use to speak explicitly to us — then we have taken a step away from being controlled by them.

---

[12] It is therefore significant how we shape our emotions by the different verbal signs we provide them for the sake of expression. For instance, if we think of our emotions in terms of "good" and "bad," then we have endowed *all* emotions with a thin veil of evaluation: satisfaction for some, and guilt/condemnation for others. That affects the way we feel our feelings — fracturing them, compounding them, complexifying them with certain glosses and judgments. For example, it changes our experience of distress if we think about the opposite of distress as *happy*, or if we think about the opposite of distress as *calm*. *Happy* is hard to manufacture. But *calm* is a more physiologically determined state by nature. The way we "cut the pie" of our emotions can determine the difference between spiraling into emotional despair, or finding a back door into peace and self-control through proper emotional self-understanding. I was personally helped by Alex Zautra's "Circumplex" model of emotions in his more academic work *Emotions, Stress, and Health* (New York: Oxford University Press, 2003), 21-25. For a simplified application of this principle applied to stress, I highly recommend Kelly McGonigal's TED Talk "How To Make Stress Your Friend" (June 2013). https://www.ted.com/talks/kelly_mcgonigal_how_to_make_stress_your_friend?language=e n. Accessed on July 30th, 2016.

Uniquely for Twentysomethings

This book is uniquely for twentysomethings, because our third decade is when we become responsible for our emotions for the first time — when we can't pass them off on someone else, when we must face *the feeling*, without the ability to change the circumstance which it is about.

If we do not learn the skills required to *feel* responsibly, then our third decade will become the decade which our emotions were granted authority over willpower — when our ability to tell ourselves what to do collapsed. It is in this decade that we must shift our difficult decision to be spiritually and cognitively virtuous into second gear, because if we don't, we will spend the rest of our lives making other people take responsibility for our emotions. And that is a terrible prison that holds many intimate relationships hostage until death. This book is intended to function as a real-time prison break.

Resisting "Life Hacks" and "Jesus Jukes"

We must — those of us wondering if we will make it to our thirtieth birthday alive, or sane — resist the secular allure of treating our complex existential dilemmas with solutions that we can buy and sell — solutions that can be listed in … well, a list. Any practical theology that can accurately be called a "life hack" sacrifices theology for practice, and thereby sacrifices the practical for the illusion of practicality.

We must also resist the notion that preaching Christ is sufficient to address the darkness. We must ask ourselves: how can we differentiate our *serious* Christian exhortations in the name of Christ, from what we call in jest "Jesus jukes?"

Aristotle called it bad poetry. The ancient term for Jesus juke was *deus ex machina* — "God from the machine" — and it denoted the contrived appeal to the divine, pretending that merely bringing God into the picture adequately addressed the complexity of the tragedy.[13] In ancient tragedies, characters in trouble would be whisked off with a crane, caught up by the gods. How often do we expect our theology to do the work of a crane, whisking away our emotions and troubles and cares, thus mechanically ascending our imaginations to Jesus Christ?

It's easy to prefer the neatly ruled margins of our journaling bibles to the abyss which threatens us with emotions too big for us. In order to trust God, must we believe that he will act today as the pagan gods of the Greek tragedies? Will God save us — by contrivance, by fiat — without concern for the warp and woof of our lives in which we are firmly situated?

Any practical theology that can accurately be called a "Jesus juke" sacrifices practice for theology, and thereby sacrifices true theology for the illusion of the theological.

The best practical theology will uncover the connection between our darkest moments and the person of Christ himself, without capitulating to the cowardice of life-hacks or Jesus-jukes. We never know when circumstances will turn to quicksand, or when God will surprise us with his saving. But, to practice our theology, we walk forward in the minefield of life, knowing that the shrapnel is real and painful, learning that God's saving is far more profound than whisking us away with a crane.

Commencement

Many books for twentysomethings are pandering and self-interested. Nearly all of them have turned into online revenue-generating video classes that promise to help buyers "get unstuck," "find

---

[13] See Aristotle, *Poetics* New York: Penguin, 1996), liii (11.5). Antiphanes, an ancient Athenian playwright, notes: "Moreover, when tragedians are not able to say any more and are absolutely at an impasse in their plays, they raise up the crane just like a finger, and the audience is satisfied." Plato likewise comments: "Just as the authors of tragedy, whenever they are at a loss in some way, take refuge in the use of the crane, raising gods aloft." Donald J. Mastronarde, *The Art of Euripides: Dramatic Technique and Social Context* (New York: Cambridge University Press, 2010), 181. It would serve us well to be left unsatisfied by these sorts of contrivances, with the playwrights, apart from the audience's ears itching for resolution as quickly as possible — when does resolution ever come so quickly?

themselves," and "break out."

I don't think that's the kind of book you want, because that's not the kind of book I want. I want a serious engagement with the issues that dominate my crisis — depression, loneliness, suicidality — and I simply hadn't found a book that did so in a compelling or excellent way. I want this to be a book you can use for yourself, or give to a friend, or give to a parent or partner who doesn't quite understand what you're going through.

This book is intended to help you feel your way through the unlit basement of life. I hope that you find the book easy to navigate, and to implement into your search for healing, for growth, and for God. I hope this book can serve as a step forward in the search, in the journeying, in the trusting, for both of us.

My Gratitude

Thank you for reading this book. Thank you for trusting me with your time, with your ear, with your heart. I've done my best to write something that will repay your time with value.

> *Lord, do in us that thing*
> *which we are scared*
> *might be impossible:*
>
> *Heal us.*
> *Change us.*
> *Restore us.*
> *Grow us up.*
> *Unburden us.*
> *Release us from sin.*
> *Help us to feel okay.*
> *Help us to get control.*
> *Help us to live another day.*
> *Help us to breathe another breath,*
> *   after we've been kicked in the stomach.*
>
> *Do what we can't do.*
> *…what only you can do.*

We pray this in the name of the one for whom
"there was no place" (Luke 2:7),
Jesus Christ. Amen.

Chapter 1
Quarter Life Crisis

To have despaired, have hoped, believed,
And been for evermore beguiled;
…
Was ever darkness like to this?[1]
  —William Wordsworth

The human body starts dying at age 25. Our twenties slap us with the expiration date of sin's curse (Genesis 6:3): slowly, in our ligaments; tightly, in our muscle fibers; subtly, checking for bumps; decimally, with a rising BMI. We feel death in our twenties; emotionally and relationally, in ugly and odious ways. Death latches its chain to our frame, slowly pulling us deep into an answer to the question "Death, where is your sting?" (1 Corinthians 15:55). Our twenties bring so many answers to that question — transition, failure, desperation, dependence, accusation, responsibility, moral failure, stagnation, unfulfillment. "Sting" isn't sufficient. Our twenties can be a dark time.

> **Definition:**
>
> *Our quarter life crisis is a season when we realize:*
> *We are promised no earthly thing in this life.*

---

[1] William Wordsworth, "The Affliction of Margaret —," in *The Complete Poetical Works of William Wordsworth* (New York: Macmillan and Co., 1893), 206 [205-206].

Five Aspects of Our Quarter-Life Crisis

Like an immigrant landing on the shores of a new country, our third decade throws us into the midst of chaotic realities that are beyond us. We have always wanted to grow up. We have always wanted to have the benefits of being adults. We have always wanted to be free from our parents, our limitations, accelerating fearlessly into the lives we have always imagined. And, like an ambush, new voices emerge from dark corners we never knew about.

1. Disappointment

"I thought things would be better."
"I thought I would be better."
"I thought friendships would stay together."

We show up at the doorstep of our twenties and mid-twenties hoping to meet our childhood dreams. It turns out that we oversold ourselves on our future. No astronaut missions. No presidencies. No spouse and kids. No house. "Wait, does life suck?" Expectations aren't shown to be false — only shown to be miniature scales of what we're actually hoping for; financially in dire straights, emotionally unfulfilled, professionally unimpressive, and spiritually stagnant. "I thought I would have grown out of this sin by now." Shared, white-walled apartment spaces drag our nerves with doom: "This can't be it. This can't be all there is." The doors of childhood are closed behind. Life, it seems, indicates that things will only be getting worse from here.

2. Despondency

"I'm just not as happy as I used to be."
"I feel fundamentally unable to see the bright side of life."
"My ability to feel joy is just broken."

Each day — another day, and another — erodes the soul. Each day, a little less meaningful, a little more hazy; a few less moments of true beauty, a few more innocent pleasures to make it through.

Unrelenting haze. Emotional nebula. Spiritual indolence. Slowly — down, sinking — down, twisting — down. Lethargic weight, myopic gaze. "Darkness" is not a sufficient word. Heavy. Weary. Vapid. Unaroused. Despondent.

3. Despair

"Nothing I do matters."
"I'm going to be stuck here forever."
"My parents are so disappointed."
"All of my friends are doing so much better than I am."
"Life just feels like a rat race."

Despair is the emotional muscle of "Oh God, this will never end." Pay up. You're bulldozed. Despair is the overdrawn bank account — "Insufficient hope. Please deposit more faith to make a withdrawal." And we have nothing. Rejection letters, romantic break ups, deaths of parents and siblings, bad news tailor fit to our most arresting anxieties. They've embarrassed us with empty hands. They are thieves of hope. Ruthless pillagers of dreams. Our circumstances, emotions, and relationships — we are fooling ourselves if we don't think they are interwoven in the fabric of our beliefs. And when they die, despair comes alive.

4. Doubt

"The church doesn't understand or address the issues I'm struggling with."
"I feel judged by God all the time."
"I'm not sure that God exists. And if he does, I don't care."

Doubt has been consecrated and crowned by the millennial generation of twentysomethings — hail, our new priest and king: incredulity. "God, if your people are so loving, then why . . ." "God, if you're so great, then why . . ." "God, if you're not a sadistic, disinterested deity, then why . . ." As we sink deeper into despondency, we lock arms with doubt. Our faith turns from "He will come again" to "That one time when . . ." — from "I believe" to "I once believed."

5. Desolation

"I haven't felt God in a really long time."
"Friends are fake."
"I don't have a place that feels like home."

Desolation — "Anguished misery or loneliness; a state of complete emptiness or destruction" — from the Latin *desolare*, "to abandon." Loneliness can be the most crushing force in the universe. The heartache of leaving home requires more than wisdom and a coffee table — it can take and contort and dismember the soul. To lose for the first time the holding hand, the loving concern, the caring eye, the steady help — it can be grievous. Alone; therefore, alone forever; therefore, helpless. To be desolated is to be broken by the void. And we are being broken.

God and the Darkness of Our Twenties

God was a twentysomething once — Christ in the flesh. But there is more. He created twentysomething-ness. He died for twentysomethings and was raised for twentysomethings. I know, I know. *It's irrelevant. It doesn't change anything. Jesus Christ doesn't change anything,* you might think.

Leslie Newbigin said, "I am neither an optimist nor a pessimist; Jesus Christ is risen from the dead." Is Jesus irrelevant? How is wallowing in a dialectic of self-deprecation and self-pity going? Is that doing things for you? Is that doing more than Jesus has done? If so, close this book. Get off the Internet. Go and drink and at the very least be merry, for tomorrow you die (1 Corinthians 15:32). But if you're clawing for a grip — for something, anything — keep reading. Jesus actually changes quite a bit. Here are five things he offers.

1. Diligence

"I'm going to own this."

Responsibilities are scorching. Perhaps never more so than when we first feel their heat, and that they will never end. In order to feel a desire to move forward in a new stage in life, we have to do the hard work of letting go of our old life — a good life, as children, as carefree, as optimistic, as unjaded, as fearless and free to dream beyond our reach.

That's gone now. It's not an overstatement to say that we may need to formally grieve our childhood, so that we can leave it behind. "We're like shellfish that continue to open and close their shells on the tide schedule of their home waters after they have been transplanted to a laboratory tank or the restaurant kitchen" (William Bridges, "Transition"). We need to acclimate to our new surroundings.

In a dark and depressing transition, Ezra "made confession, weeping and casting himself down" (Ezra 10:1). The people gave him a mission — to make space for God: "Arise, for it is your task, and we are with you; be strong and do it" (Ezra 10:4). Before anything else, we need one thing in our twenties: a meaningful task. It's part of our constitution as human beings — to seek and yearn for and mourn the absence of a meaningful task: "aspire to live quietly, and to mind your own affairs, and to work with your hands, as we instructed you" (1 Thessalonians 4:11).

Diligence sets the necessary rhythm for the gospel to weave its way into the crippling emotions that our twenties can bring. Diligence in grief, in moving on, in acclimating, in moving forward — diligence in meaning is the fundamental counteragent to the quarterlife crisis.

2. Dreams

"I'm here because you want me to be here.
I want something else."

First, if you see the darkness as a deathblow to hope, you're already dead. There is no overcoming the darkness of despair if it meets a willing heart. But it is not a deathblow. Despair is a gauntlet thrown — here, in our twenties, we must learn the guerilla violence of the Christian life. "Do not go gentle into that good night. Rage, rage against the dying of the light." There are no points for style. Despair is not a prophet or friend — despair always speaks with a froward tongue, and it deserves bloody brutality.

This is not a macho thing. It is a life-in-the-Spirit thing. Jeremiah's prophet Baruch cried, "Woe is me! For the Lord has added sorrow to my pain. I am weary with my groaning, and I find no rest" (Jeremiah 45:3). God responds, "I will give you your life as a prize of war in all places to which you may go" (Jeremiah 45:5). God fights with us, if we will fight. The apostle John writes to the young because "you have overcome the evil one" and because "you are strong" (1 John 2:13–14).

Second, those dark feelings might not be so dark. They might actually mean something. They may be a flashing red warning: "Do that other thing." Or "Don't settle here forever." Paul insists: "Let each person lead the life that the Lord has assigned to him, and to which God has called him" (1 Corinthians 7:17). Are you following the dreams of your parents? Your community? Are your dreams a slave to your fears? The intimacy of our individual union with Christ allows us the freedom to stop living other people's dreams. God has given you a personal call. It's okay to take a risk on your own, and dream big for the glory of God.

3. Dissatisfaction

"I can't just give up."

Are you dissatisfied? Good. The world is full of feasts that satiate the flesh in the moment, but starve the soul.[2] Believe better about yourself than "this present evil age" (Galatians 1:4). If we believe the world's message that we are incomplete, inadequate, insufficient just to the degree that we can fix it — with enough Facebook, with enough money, with enough sex, with enough hobbies — then we are slaves to those things (Romans 6:16).[3] We are both more hopeless, and have

---

[2] "It is better to go to the house of mourning than to go to the house of feasting, for this is the end of all mankind, and the living will lay it to heart" (Ecclesiastes 7:2). Any version of Christianity that withholds this verse from you because of certain expectations on your emotional life is less than biblical. And any version of Christianity built solely on this passage will not remain in the last day, when mourning is turned into feasting. But today, and perhaps in this season, feasting — satisfaction — is not appropriate.

[3] "Do you not know that if you present yourselves to anyone as obedient slaves, you are slaves of the one whom you obey, either of sin, which leads to death, or of obedience, which leads to righteousness?" (Romans 6:16) Paul is not merely saying that we are undisciplined. He is saying that, outside of Christ, we are subject totally and completely to the exploitation of the powers of sin at work in the world, through all the daily technologies by which we habitually relinquish control.

more reason to hope, than we would ever imagine. God endorses your dissatisfaction with the world's self-concept package: "Large, with a side of self-doubt and a sprinkle of guilt — hold the Jesus." How predictably joyless.

Self-hatred is self-perpetuating — it is not an isolated thought; it is a downward and accelerating cycle. We judge our desires: incomplete, unaccomplished, base, stupid, unrealistic. Don't try to preempt your disappointment and abandonment with self-condemnation and self-abandonment. It is a cycle into a numb and catatonic existence. Find the fire. Our twenties can be an anesthesia — they can numb us to pain and motivation. If we can stop the morphine drip of despondency, we will find that our unbearable existential angst is not a prophet of doom — it is the pain of depressurization, rising out of the depths. "I was brutish and ignorant; I was like a beast toward you. Nevertheless, I am continually with you; you hold my right hand" (Psalm 73:22–23). Dissatisfaction is what God uses to separate us from the beasts.

4. Dependence

"I *am* okay."

God is a loving Father. Full stop. Part of that package: God cares about your parental issues. If you had an abusive, disappointing, harmful, traumatizing, or maladaptive relationship with your parents, that is a tragedy and a burden. And yet, God — your perfect Father — cares for you, and cares about your story. David Powlison explains, "Dynamic psychology [turns] the antique relationship with parents into a magic wand to explain all of life. The Bible offers . . . a more concrete and life-transforming explanation."[4]

God does not expect you to be a Wall Street executive. God does not wish you were making six figures. God does not wish you had a happy-go-lucky personality. God does not wish you would just "Get yourself together already!" We are not on our own. We are not broken

---

[4] David Powlison, "What if Your Father Didn't Love You?" *The Journal of Biblical Counseling* 7, no. 1 (1993): 6 [2–7].

beyond repair. We are not doomed to be our parents.[5]. We are not condemned by our heavenly Father for being in process: "Count the patience of our Lord as salvation" (2 Peter 3:15). God knows us and loves us and is working patiently in and with us: "I write to you, children, because you know the Father" (1 John 2:13). You can depend on him for love, affirmation, affection, correction, a guiding hand, and his never-forsaking care. Breathe.

5. Devotion

"God, help me. I need your help."

God is devoted to us. That may sound strange — aren't we devoted to God? Isn't "devoted" an inferior activity? No. God is devoted to Christ and we are one with Christ: "Do not be afraid or tremble . . . God is the one who goes with you. He will not fail you or forsake you" (Deuteronomy 31:6). To the extent that God is devoted to and present with Christ, he is devoted to and present with us.[6] God will never be more devoted to us than he is today, even at his return: We have "salvation that is in Christ Jesus with eternal glory" (2 Timothy 2:10).

This may sound trite. That's okay. God doesn't promise that his truths will always carry the wit of that guy in your creative writing MFA that's putting you $25,000 in debt. God says trite things — God repeats one single, unoriginal, overstated, overplayed truth again and again because we forget it just as often: "Work, for I am with you" (Haggai 2:4). "I am with you always, to the end of the age" (Matthew 28:20). "The Lord is near to the brokenhearted" (Psalm 34:18).

---

[5] For example, Amon did exactly as his father Menassah had done — worshipping idols an oppressing his people (2 Kings 21:19–26), whereas Amon's son Josiah turned from the ways of Menassah and worshipped God, restoring Israel to its rightful place as a God-worshipping people, despite his family history (2 Kings 22:2).

[6] "And he put all things under his feet and gave him as head over all things to the church, which is his body, the fullness of him who fills all in all (Ephesians 1:22-23)."

Conclusion

God is with the lonely and the heartbroken. "Where? Where is he?" He is . . . he is there. Sometimes there is more to say, and sometimes there is not. You object: "Reproaches have broken my heart, so that I am in despair. I looked for pity, but there was none, and for comforters, but I found none" (Psalm 69:20). He will not stop repeating: "He who touches you touches the apple of his eye" (Zechariah 2:8). He embarks with us on this journey that feels lonely and unforgiving and emotionally brutal. "But how?" Let's take it one brutal emotion at a time.

Chapter 2
Depression

> The misery and splendor of human life
> fit no simplistic explanation.[1]
>   —Walter Brueggemann

My depression is constantly shifting — muddled, dragging me from laziness to activity; from checking out to clocking in. Depression bullies me from place to place, from extreme to extreme.

Depression has littered lots of painful verbs on my floor: stranded, sleeping, forgetting, screaming, choking, drowning, suffocating, imploding, crying, hugging, torturing.[2] Yes, these are the present-tense words that orbit the depressed heart in its silent, sober noon hours. The sunlight mocks you when depressed — bright, enlightening, warming, everything you aren't; brightening the world you find cold and unwelcoming, force-feeding your imagination with hearty joy that your soul's sickness cannot tolerate or digest.[3]

---

[1] William Wordsworth, "Surprised By Joy — Impatient as the Wind," *The Sonnets of William Wordsworth* (London: Edward Moxon, 1838), 31.

[2] The term *depression*, coined by Swiss-born Adolf Meyer of Johns Hopkins Medical School, "has slithered innocuously through the language like a slug, leaving little trace of its intrinsic malevolence and preventing, by its very insipidity, a general awareness of the horrible intensity of the disease when out of control." William Styron, *Darkness Visible: A Memoir of Madness* (New York: Vintage Books, 1992), 36.

[3] Emily Dickenson knows the intolerable way that sunlight expands sadness: "There's a certain Slant of light, / Winter Afternoons – / That oppresses, like the Heft / Of Cathedral Tunes – " Sharon Leiter comments, "Dickinson's astonishing feat in this poem is that she somehow transforms light, an image deeply embedded in the human psyche as an emblem of joy, hope, happiness, and salvation, into the 'Seal' that signifies existential despair and locks it within the soul." Sharon Lieter, *Critical Companion to Emily Dickinson: A Literary Reference to Her Life and Work* (New York: Infobase, 2007), 197.

Depression is a disease.[4] Even saying that feels too sanitized —
we forget that diseases are noxious and vulgar organisms that hack and
deform our bodies. Depression malforms our nervous system, like a
cocktail of adrenalin and anesthetic laced into our daily affections.
William Styron describes it as "the gray drizzle of horror," a despair
which resembles "the diabolical discomfort of being imprisoned in a
fiercely overheated room."[5]

Five Aspects of Our Depression

Dictionaries resort to a cluster of synonyms for "sadness" in order to
define depression. These definitions are too on-the-nose. If we say,
"Depression is sadness!" we have taken zero helpful steps forward. We
will therefore outsource our definition of depression to an insider.

> ## Definition:
>
> *Depression is "just this detached, meaningless fog
> where you can't feel anything about anything."[6]*

That's a good expansion. Depression *is* sadness. But it is dejection and
detachment and all these one-inch-removed words, too. We need this
definition, because depression is a deep, dark, bottomless chasm that
refuses to be tidied up — everything that makes us *us* is swallowed up by
the creeping cardiac paralysis of depression. *That* is the starting point

---

[4] "Illness of the mind is real illness." Andrew Solomon, *The Noonday Demon: An
Atlas of Depression* (New York: Scribner, 2001), 7. John Piper agrees with Richard
Baxter that depression is a disease, in "When the Darkness Does Not Lift," *When I
Don't Desire God* (Wheaton, IL: Crossway, 2013, 2nd ed), 210.

[5] "And because no breeze stirs this caldron, because there is no escape from this
smothering confinement, it is entirely natural that the victim begins to think ceaselessly
of oblivion." Styron, *Darkness Visible*, 50.

[6] Allie Brosh, *Hyperbole and a Half: Unfortunate Situations, Flawed Coping
Mechanisms, Mayhem, and Other Things That Happened* (New York: Touchstone,
2013), 128. You really owe it to yourself to read both chapters in this book on
depression. Her pictures perfectly express depression in ways that no words ever can.

with this disease: you have no answer. Start there, and you begin to understand.

Let's take a look at five aspects of the depressed heart.

1. Guilt and Shame

> "I deserve to be sad. Look at all my sin."
> "Joy in God ... a blessing for the obedient."
> "After this morning, last night, last week ...
>   I'll settle for my cycle of sadness as penance."

The roots of depression grow strong in the soil of self-blame. We hear the command to rejoice — we know that good Christians rejoice! — but ... you can't. You're pressing the right buttons and nothing is happening. Prayer, nothing. Bible, nothing. Friends, nothing. Church, even worse — here, you can *see* all the happy people that you're not.[7] And you can't help but offer an explanation for your deficiency: you are suffering, and you have earned it. God is the schoolmaster, and depression is the whipped ruler — *snap*, right on the knuckles of your soul. Depression is our overzealous disciplinarian: "Major depression is far too stern a teacher: you needn't go to the Sahara to avoid frostbite."[8]

2. Numbness

> "I wish I could cry
> as easy as the sky. The tears don't come
> as easily now. They're
> stuck inside my soul."[9]

---

[7] It's even worse for the abused, who will assume that any sense of unbelonging is both deserved and divine: Jutta Lindert, et al., "Sexual and Physical Abuse in Childhood is Associated with Depresison and Anxiety Over the Life Course: Systematic Review and Meta-Analysis," *International Journal of Public Health* 59, no. 2 (2014): 359–372.

[8] Andrew Solomon, *The Noonday Demon: An Atlas of Depression* (New York: Scribner, 2001), 434.

[9] A prayer by Angel, in Andrew Solomon, *The Noonday Demon: An Atlas of Depression* (New York: Scribner, 2001), 425.

In bed, watching TV, eating cereal, which is of course making you fat — a further reason not to journey beyond the boundaries of your house. Depression is an entire arsenal of concrete shoes, fixing you to the ground, letting you witness the world but not participate. And every second you resign to the full reality of depression gets thrown on the stack of evidence: "You'll never escape. See how long you've been stuck here?" Every hour you stay in bed, every tequila shot you take, every whole pizza you eat, weighs about a thousand pounds: "*Merrrh.*"

Allie Brosh helps us here:

> "It's weird for people who still have feelings to be around depressed people. They try to help you have feelings again so things can go back to normal, and it's frustrating for them when that doesn't happen. From their perspective, it seems like there has *got* to be some untapped source of happiness within you that you've simply lost track of, and if you could just see how beautiful things are ..."[10]

3. Self-Pity

> "I'm completely alone."
> "People who 'love' me really just feel bad for me."
> "This is going to last forever."

You feel crazy. Well-meaning loved-ones quip, "Pick yourself up!" which only concretizes your defensive posture about your depression. You have the *right* to be depressed ... right? Well, after months (or years) of unending emotional suffering, the unspoken "If I could be happy, *I would*" sticks a little more sharply into your relationships.

4. Bleakness

> "Maybe you should rejoice in Christ a little more."
> "Maybe you should look on the bright side."
> "Maybe you should be a little more normal."
> "Have you tried remembering all the
> good things God has done for you?"

---

[10] Allie Brosh, 127.

For the depressed, beauty is only painful.[11] Like emotional rabies, hacking and spitting out the elements that nourish our soul because they are unpalatable to us, depression chokes the brain of beauty.[12] And that slides under the radar of Christianity as sober piety long enough. Luminescent love lies on the floor, ashen, drab and drooping, folding one day after another into the fetal position.

5. Degradation

Routine sadness drags us cyclically downhill (especially disproportionate sadness). We calculate that we can afford depression in our souls — that the death grip it has on us won't cost us much. But it takes us hostage, and each day, conforms us into its likeness. A little more lopsided, a little more tightly twisted in knots, running the soul's engine a little to hot for its own good, daily until growing deformity feels normal. Depression displays the full meaning of iniquity — bending the spine of our souls backward, titanic in criticism and embryonic in contentment.

Eventually, when your sadness takes as prisoner your joy and innocence and childhood self, then depression starts getting labeled disobedience. You no longer know if you struggle with depression or rage. Or perhaps you only feel the departing shadow of those feelings, whimpering and withering somewhere inside you, never certain if their silence is emotional atrophy or rigor mortis.

God and Our Noonday Demon

When we first became Christians, we had all these wonderful emotions — like heirloom Christmas tree ornaments on our soul, the gospel felt as if it had finally given shape and appeal to our searching and our pain. Our fretting over our smallness was chastened, and replaced

---

[11] Depression experiences the entire world as a barren wasteland, blind to beauty and dead to awe, peace entirely dimmed and diminished: "The grass was scanty, coarse, and grey; and the leaves in the thickets were faded and failing. It was a cheerless land, and their journey was slow and gloomy." J. R. R. Tolkien, *The Fellowship of the Ring* (New York: Mariner, 2005), 225.

with satisfaction. God built a real temple inside us, where we could go with prayer and Bible reading and fellowship.

And then, depression came.

We became confused. Aren't we supposed to be happy and smiling? Doesn't Jesus just make you want to cry tears of joy? Yes, he certainly did once. Well, now ... it's hard to cry tears of anything when that place you used to feel warmth and pain and meaning is lying in your chest cavity with its tongue out and X's for eyes, lifeless and limp and shriveled and dead. What does the Christian life look like then — when your heart dies before your body?

1. Lament

"God, I'm not okay."

It is too easy to rob lament from the Christian. But that thievery steals not only from the Christian life, but from Scripture. The only way we will see the way Christ truly encounters the depressed is if we stop insisting that he must tie everything up neatly for us at the end, with a nice little bow:

> "Yes, pain is deep.
>> But God is good."
> "Yes, life is hard.
>> But the wood of the cross was hard."
> "Yes, you are brokenhearted.
>> But 'God heals the brokenhearted' — Psalm 147:3."

What do all of these things have in common? They all intolerantly push against the legitimacy of lament, as if it were the lesser genre of Scripture — like Neptune, still part of our Bible's solar system, but furthest from the gospel's warming sun (sorry, Pluto). That may be the very point. Perhaps what the Bible gives us in its gift of lament, which humans and Christians together want to rush past as quickly as possible, is a cold

---

[12] "Ach! No! ... You try to choke poor Sméagol. Dust and ashes, he can't eat that. He must starve. But Sméagol doesn't mind. Nice hobbits! Sméagol has promised. He will starve. He can't eat hobbits' food. He will starve. Poor thin Sméagol!" J. R. R. Tolkien, *The Two Towers* (New York: Del Ray, 2012), 255.

planet that gives appropriate expression to their pain.

The author of Lamentations is caught in a psychological tug-of-war between conviction and emotion. God authored every single one of these words, uttered from the mouth of the same human, in the same inspired book:

- My soul is bereft of peace;
  I have forgotten what happiness is. (Lam 3:17)
- The steadfast love of the LORD never ceases;
  his mercies never come to an end. (Lam. 3:22)
- The Lord has swallowed up
  without mercy. (Lam 2:2)
- Why do you forget us forever;
  why do you forsake us for so many days? (Lam. 5:20)

God gave these words to us. We rush past them. We cherry pick "his mercies never come to an end" in order to helicopter out of Lamentations into some exuberant Psalm.

We rush to the end of the prayer, to the end of the grief, to the end of the lament, to the end of the Bible … "But …. but *Jesus!*" What we proclaim as a Christian community — *maranatha* – "Come, Lord Jesus" — and we have made our prayer into our implicit permission to pretend as if there is no real "not yet" to his coming.[13] We feel the pressure to finish every lament with evangelical consolation. If we can't finish the sentence with a relieved tone, we fear we are doing a disservice to the gospel.

---

[13] Herman Ridderbos explains: "The certainty that in Christ the day of salvation … has dawned does not mean the end of redemptive expectation, but only makes it increase in intensity." Herman Ridderbos, *Paul: An Outline of His Theology*, trans. John Richard De Witt (Grand Rapids, MI: Eerdmans, 1975), 487. Thus, the reality of the hope and joy secured for us by Christ does not *necessarily* give us the thing toward which our hope is pointed in this age, but makes us lament all the louder as we see that we don't have it. We sense, increasingly every day, how impoverished our souls are until we are given in practice what has been granted to us in principle by God in Christ. We must resist the urge to pretend and impose on the church the notion that we have presently all that God has promised us. Certainly, we do not: 'Affliction' … very definitely characterizes the last phase of the present world preceding the coming of Christ." Ridderbos, *Paul*, 488. This state of affairs does not foil our hope, but is the very precondition for it: "Now faith is the assurance of things hoped for, the conviction of things not seen" (Hebrews 11:1). Could we also call faith "The assertion of things hoped for, the contending for things not *felt?*"

We feel that if we can't resolve the great sorrow of the world with the cross by the end of a blog, a book, a sermon, a prayer, a conversation, then we have failed God. Nice little bows really are very pretty, after all. Is it so wrong to sign Jesus's name on the card of every experience — every death, every assault, every trauma, every tear, every suicidal thought — and call it a "gift?"[14] The Bible doesn't seem to do that. Yes, the Father gives us gifts. But there are serpents in the world as we now experience it.[15] By trying to tie everything up neatly at the end, we truly fail the depressed, about whom God cares deeply.

As depressed Christians, we feel the weight of the expectation for joy. "My friends scorn me; my eye pours out tears to God" (Job 16:20) "I hoped for happiness, but evil came; I looked for light, but there was darkness (Job 30:26). That's how the gospel can feel — like a weight, a growing shadow of condemnation that transforms our gloom from a mere diagnosis, into a divine denouncement.

We feel as if "Depressed Christian" belongs in a book under the heading "Abnormal Theology." But it is as normal as the tears of every single character in Scripture — even the divine lamenter, Jesus.

> The very nature of lament "is constant and durative. An impatient, death-denying society demands that sufferers 'get over it.' . . . In this life [there] are things for which there's no getting over; such belong to the land of lament. With maturity, by God's grace, the scales of woe and trust become balanced. In the meanwhile, we pray that e shall rejoice over deliverance yet to come, as we adorn the graves of the dead and loved and remembered. . . . lament is not an occasional tune, hummed by

---

[14] "Every good gift and every perfect gift is from above, coming down from the Father of lights with whom there is no variation or shadow due to change" (James 1:17). Notice, while every good thing is from God, not every thing that comes our way is a good thing from the hand of God's fatherly care (James 1:13–16). In fact, the very thrust of the text is that those who attribute *everything* to God directly in order to call it "good" are "deceived."

[15] "The God of peace will soon crush Satan under your feet. The grace of our Lord Jesus Christ be with you" (Romans 16:20).

others. It has become the signature theme of every life in Christ."[16]

Jesus wails. Jesus ugly cries. Jesus takes issue with his experience, and directs his displeasure toward God in prayer — "Why have you forsaken me?" (Matthew 27:46) "Father, if you are willing, remove this cup from me" (Luke 22:42). Cycle through the prayers of Jesus and the prayers of Lamentations above. Find your words, and perhaps, if God's mercies really do never come to an end, you will come to that most desired place where you can feel again, where you can cry for the first time in … you don't even know how long. Lament, with Scripture and with Christ:

> Why have you forsaken me?
> I don't even know what "happiness" is anymore.
> Why does it feel like you have left *for good*?
> Take this *nothingness* from me.
> When you say "God," my soul says "merciless."

> …

> You never stop loving me.
> Your mercies never come to an end.

2. Meaning

"There is meaning to be found here."

The most intolerable pain is trivialized pain — no perceivable greater purpose, no "it all works out" floating on the surface. Just circumstantial slop, clogging our lives, preventing us from experiencing God and love and everything beautiful. But to despair for lack of meaning is a fool's escape from the battle with depression. There is *always* meaning. Qoheleth, the "Teacher" who authored the book of Ecclesiastes, unfolds

[16] C. Clifton Black, "The Persistence of Wounds," *Lament: Reclaiming Practices in Pulpit, Pew, and Public Square*, ed. Sally A. Brown and Patrick D. Miller (Louisville, KY: Westminster John Jnox, 2005), 55 [47-58]. Ellen T. Charry comments further: "Hope only intensifies the psychological distress, the jarring effect of having things erupt in one's face when tragedy strikes." Ellen T. Charry, "May We Trust God and (Still) Lament? Can We Lament and (Still) Trust God?" *Lament: Reclaiming Practices in Pulpit, Pew, and Public Square*, ed. Sally A. Brown and Patrick D. Miller (Louisville, KY: Westminster John Jnox, 2005), 96 [95-108].

his psychological back-and-forth between joy and despair in a threefold process:

Your End Looms With Despair:

Let a man remember
    the days of darkness,
For there will be many.
      All that comes is vanity.
      (Ecclesiastes 11:8).

Your longevity will bring more painful days than you can imagine. You will feel "like butter that has been scraped over too much bread."[17] That's neither palatable to your ears, nor comforting to your soul. It is bitter and harsh like slapping frozen hands with a whip in a snowstorm. This passage feels callous and inhuman. But emotional misery has deeper value than our hearts, to which we desire God to brownnose, can often intuit.

Your Beginning Lingers With Joy:

Rejoice, O young man, in your youth,
    And let your heart cheer you in the days of your youth.
Walk in the ways of your heart
    And the sight of your eyes.
    (Ecclesiastes 11:9)

Being depressed about the unending future is the wrong "path" to take the meaning of misery. Misery, in a backwards way, does not prompt us to despair, but to *long* for joy. "Correct remembering of the days to come prompts one to enjoy. If remembering the days to come brings only misery, one must *not* remember the days to come."[18]

    Like waking up leisurely on a Saturday morning, only to have the moment spoiled by the thought that Monday is two days away, depression has a way of dumping future misery into our present joy, cancelling it out. We must never forget, whether in the context of misery or pleasure, that God has created us for joy, and that pain exists to highlight and embellish moments and seasons of joy.

---

[17] J. R. R. Tolkien, *The Fellowship of the Ring* (New York: Del Ray, 2012), 34.
[18] Choon-Leong Seow, *Ecclesiastes*, The Anchor Yale Bible Commentaries (New York: Yale University Press, 1997), 53.

God Lingers With You:
But know that for all these things
God will bring you into judgment.
Remove vexation from your heart,
And put away pain from your body,
For youth and the dawn of life are vanity.
(Ecclesiastes 11:9-10)

The cycle of game and work, ease and exertion, relaxing Saturdays and rock-splitting Mondays is, in its entirety, with all its emotional entailments, comes directly from the hand of God. "Qoheleth's affirmation of joy is an expression of the doctrine of creation. . . . This is not hedonism in the context of despair, but an affirmation of life as God has made it."[19]

Rightly facing the darkness of depression is a matter of rightly receiving the gift of life *as a whole* from God as he has given it. Can we control whether we are depressed? Sometimes, yes. Other times, no. Can we control whether we are affected deeply by depression's meaning? Absolutely not.[20] But we can control whether we *remember* its meaning. And perhaps, if we have the grit to remember, it is that loop of remembrance that will synchronize us into a cycle of steady growth.

3. Correction

"There is a door that leads out of this place."

The notion of "correcting depression" sounds harsh to our 21st century ears, which are attuned to the key of victimhood culture which panders to suffering, which dramatizes all of reality to the sufferer's key. "They love the truth for the light it sheds but hate it when it shows them up as being wrong."[21] But even antidepressants and therapy are forms of "corrective" treatment — we don't want to rebuke the depressed person

---

[19] Craig G. Bartholomew, "Book of Ecclesiastes," in *Dictionary for Theological Interpretation of the Bible*, ed. Kevin J. Vanhoozer (Grand Rapids, MI: Baker Academic, 2005), 184 [182-185].

[20] Even Jesus, in facing his own death, did not have complete command over what he felt, according to B. B. Warfield, who comments on Gethsemane: "the clearly realized approach of his death . . . threw him inwardly into profound agitation." B. B. Warfield, "On the Emotional Life of our Lord," *Biblical and Theological Studies*, edited by B. B. Warfield, et al. (New York: Charles Scribner's Sons, 1922), 73.

[21] Augustine, *Confessions*, 10.23.34.

for their suffering, yet we recognize there is a need for some proactive change.

God offers the sort of correction which objective medicine cannot offer: *evaluative correction*. "Grief is depression in proportion to circumstance; depression is grief out of proportion to circumstance."[22] God calls our disproportionate sadness what it is — improper and hypersensitive. We buck at such rebuke. We would prefer self-soothing platitudes that render life in terms of our depression, rather than the other way around.

> I calmed myself until morning;
> like a lion he breaks all my bones;
> from day to night you bring me to an end.
> (Isaiah 38:13)

Our hearts are self-soothing and self-destructive ... and never merely pathological. And God's saving of our hearts, as an active and passive organ, is both active and passive — God treats both our pathologies and our doxologies, with suffering and worshiping.

God enters into the uncomfortable role of the despised practitioner, who names depression what it is — unbelonging and unwelcome. Correction feels cruel — "I would *not* be depressed if I had a choice! If anyone is responsible for my depression, God, it is *you*." The journal entry of a cornered animal. And God loves to hug cornered animals — foaming at the mouth, biting his side, drinking his blood, and being healed in his painful corrective surgery. By treating us as wounded, and by recognizing our wound of depression as an active wound which must be changed and healed, God does what no medical doctor or psychologist can do — everything.

Ed Welch recalls words spoken to a depressed friend caught in a vicious cycle of despairing self-talk, which were more helpful than all the sympathy in the world:

> "I'm going to stop you for a second. Can you hear what's happening? The more you talk, the more you despair. I can see it in you. In fact, I can feel it in myself. Here is a plan. From now on, when I see the wave of depressive and, actually, unbiblical interpretations of life crashing down on you, I am going to point

---

[22] Andrew Solomon, *The Noonday Demon: An Atlas of Depression* (New York: Scribner, 2001), 2.

it out and try to run from it with you."[23]

4. Grit

"Just. Keep. Going. Come on."

The depressed can be both unmotivated and unenthusiastic. Friends and counselors eventually become exhausted and withdraw. "I looked on the earth, and lo, it was waste and void; and to the heavens, and they had no light." (Jeremiah 4:23)

David is an exhausted depressed person. He has no time for spiritual niceties. He has no time for Christian politeness. But he makes a qualitatively different appeal:

> I am feeble and crushed;
>> I groan because of the tumult of my heart.
> O Lord, all my longing is before you;
>> my sighing is not hidden from you.
> My heart throbs; my strength fails me,
>> and the light of my eyes—it also has gone from me.
> My friends and companions stand aloof from my plague,
>> and my nearest kin stand far off.
>> (Psalm 38:8-11)

Teeth to concrete, kicked in and crushed. He feels the shrill pain of fatigue shoot throughout the fibers of his heart. "I can't do this anymore." That's why his prayer is not merely for God to move, but for God to move *quickly*:

> Do not forsake me, O LORD!
>> O my God, be not far from me!
> Make haste to help me,
>> O Lord, my salvation!
(Psalm 38:21-22)

We see a constant mantra — "I can't keep going. I can't do this forever. The thought of an endless future is unbearable — infinite days of grey, bland, haunting, shrill nothingness. It's not fair to expect this from me."

---

[23] Ed Welch, "Helping Those Who Are Depressed," *The Journal of Biblical Counseling* 18, no. 2 (2000): 25-31.

When we lose sight of Christ, the road will seem endless. "We know we will not have the stamina for it."[24] But when we look at Christ, we do not see a smile that mocks our sadness, but he who took one more step, a thousand times more than we could: "Consider him who endured such opposition from sinful men, so that you will not grow weary and lose heart" (Heb. 12:3). When we are depressed, we vomit out all the trite rejections of our sadness, because we *know* that the sadness is real. We *know* that the pessimism is somehow accurate. And Christ affirms it.

What Christ does for us is not to critique the voice which depression speaks *per se*, but he denies it the final word. The depressed feel the true, awful weight of creation's degradation into meaninglessness. Christ stiff-arms the meaningfulness of that degredation:

> We rejoice in the glory of God. Not only so, but we rejoice in our sufferings, because we know that suffering produces perseverance; perseverance, character; character, hope. And hope does not disappoint us, because God has poured out his love into our hearts by the Holy Spirit, whom he has given us. (Rom. 5:2-5)

"Perseverance? Character? Hope? No thanks." Understandable, but misguided. Depression is not merely indestructible sadness. It is pain we would never choose that God endured in order to produce the same endurance in us. "Endurance ... what a worthless gift. I don't need endurance. I need relief." We have the same concern that Paul does, and for which Jesus died — *will our hope disappoint?* Will I put one foot in front of the other again and again and again ... will it be worth it? "And hope does not disappoint us."

Now, combine this prayer with the lamenter in the Old Testament, with Jesus on the cross:

> God, please don't disappoint me.
> Restore to me the joy of your salvation (because it's *gone*).
> Will you really come through?
> Am I walking an eternal plank,
>   waiting for you to throw me to the sharks?
> Will you ever make me normal?

---

[24] Welch, "Understanding Depression," 24.

Will I ever be happy again?
Will you ever come through?

You have entered into the company of God's most beloved saints in the history of the world. As long as you are here, you are standing on holy ground.

5. Joy

"Do nothing short of the impossible: Teach me joy."

Joy. The perverted tormenter. Cackling and smiling and delighting in God, while the depressed look on in hollow longing from the margins of faith. Joy is not possible. That's why you will gag at this section. Like chemotherapy which makes us nauseous, the command for joy kills what is good and bad in us in order to save our lives. "If we idolize happiness, it will always elude us."[25] Likewise even with joy in God.
    Rejoice.

> Though the fig tree does not blossom,
>   and no fruit is on the vines;
> though the produce of the olive fails
>   and the fields yield no food;
> though the flock is cut off from the fold
>   and there is no herd in the stalls,

Say it, Habakkuk. Go ahead, say it. You will lose me. I promise.

> *yet* I will rejoice in the LORD;
>   I will exult in the God of my salvation."
>   (Habakkuk 3:17–18)

Ok, I'm still here. What happened in that verse? Some cognitive transition? Some existential realization? A moment of epiphanic ecstasy? No. None of the above. It is simply a miracle of God. It is simply "because God has poured out his love into our hearts by the Holy Spirit." (Romans 5:5). The sort of joy that Habakkuk speaks of is on the one hand the very purpose for which every human was made, and on the other hand the most impossible thing for any human will to have. Joy is a real encounter with a person, which no mental hack or mindfulness practice can achieve on its own. Real Christian joy does not force cognitive dissonance while the world slowly suffocates us — rotting our figs, stealing our food, vanishing our frail structure of wellbeing into thin air. Joy has bound us to himself, and will never let us go, no matter what we do or what we feel. Feel the impossibility?

The Christian command to rejoice is not an invitation to smile while we cry inside. Nor is it a requirement to feel something we can't force ourselves to feel. The command to "rejoice" will always, always, always feel arbitrary. As with the command to love our enemies, and to take up our cross, and to love God with all our hearts — the most fundamental realities of the Christian life are unquestionably out of our reach. There is no way around it: the Christian life *is* impossible. And the moment we forget that, we begin to walk the plank of despair.

Joy is not the strength that we bring to our Christian walk. Joy is not some feeling we muster. It is God's work, understandably absent, miraculously present, and often is a product of many moments of misery.

Can God give you joy? Yes. One of the greatest lies that depression will spin in your mind is: "This will last forever." We despair in our depression because we cannot imagine a future without it. It has become so much a part of our way of experiencing the world that we feel that it has sealed our escape hatch out into the real world where joy exists. Not joy itself, but a belief in future joy, is the grace that sustain the depressed today.
"Sometimes it is hard for us to accept that a lifetime of vigilance and running and fighting is compatible with ... joy."[26] But the most important thing the Christian can remember about joy is that *it is a process*. We are not fighting for fleeting ecstasy, but learning the skill of joy in the midst of emotional suffering. If you find yourself despairing because depression has hammered bent itself into the rebar of your soul, think of yourself as practicing piano, or lifting weights, or attempting a handstand. Joy is spontaneous, and personal, and a result of time-spent, and a product of joy-practiced:

---

[25] Ed Welch, "Understanding Depression," *The Journal of Biblical Counseling* 18, no. 2 (2000): 18 [12–24].

[26] John Piper, *Future Grace: The Purifying Power of the Promises of God*, 2nd ed. (Colorado Springs, CO: Multnomah, 2012), 314.

"People become lighter as they become stronger. As great artists perform with seeming effortlessness and can enjoy the beauty of their own artistry, people become happier as they love more supplely, enskilled by divine wisdom. This joy is the pinnacle of human happiness, theologically speaking. It may not be linear or steady progress, yet it cannot be nullified, even by adversity. Knowing that God delights as we grow from strength to strength encourages those in the light to stay the course, enjoying their participation in God's enjoyment of his cherished creation. 'May the glory of the Lord endure forever; may the Lord rejoice in his works.'"[27]

Conclusion

There are tons of little things you can do. Maybe stop listening to depressing songs for a while. Turn on some pseudo-happy music like John Mayer or Dave Matthews. Worship music always makes me sad — I think, because it makes me face my doubts about God's goodness toward me, and his disappointment about my lack of joy. But we are together in this journey. There is no possible way I can end a chapter on *de-pres-sion* and feel satisfied that you, the reader, will kick your feet up in hearty relief that results from a simple faith in Jesus Christ. Heck, *I'm not even doing that*. But I do pray that happens, for the both of us. And the race worth running is not for "the joy that Jesus wishes we had," but is the very same race that Jesus ran, which we run *with him*, "for the joy that was set before him … despising the shame" (Hebrews 12:2).

We simultaneously confess, with Allie Brosh, that depression feels like a "miserable, boring wasteland in front of you might stretch all the way into forever,"[28] and with Richard Gaffin that "we are and have already been made a part of in Christ by his Spirit."[29]

---

[27] Ellen Charry, *God and the Art of Happiness* (Grand Rapids, MI: Eerdmans, 2010), 277. Charry also insists that this process cannot be completed in this life: "Enjoying God in the beauty of holiness is possible in this life, but it cannot be complete. Happiness can only be perfected when we are no longer able to fall short of loving as we would. Therefore, sanctification now is toward glorification, when love is perfected and none shall make us afraid." Ibid., 276-277.

[28] Brosh, *Hyperbole and a Half*, 154.

[29] Richard B. Gaffin, Jr., *Paul and the Order of Salvation* (Phillipsburg, NJ: P&R Publishing, 2013, 2nd ed.), 89.

Chapter 3
Loneliness

"...the night can be a dreadful time
for lonely people once their
loneliness has started."
—Ernest Hemingway[1]

God begins his most barefaced treatment of grief, with loneliness:

How lonely sits the city
that was full of people! ...
She weeps bitterly at night ...
she has none to comfort her (Lam. 1:1-2)

We would tranquilize our loneliness, with alcohol or
pornography, with meet-ups and date nights, with friends' assurances
and self-assurances. But they all, like plastic forks in a sword fight, leave
us lacerated and broken: "I'm all alone." We don't come to that place
often, because we have so many little hacks to keep us bobbing up to the
surface of the world for distraction. But there are those moments, where
the most clear and irrefutable truth in the universe is that we are
incurably isolated — existentially homeless, loveless, socially destitute,
misunderstood and rejected by everyone we come into contact with.

You are a lonely dot in existence, going to church, attending
class, working a job, laughing with friends, and all the while, you are
invisible to your own belonging.

---

[1] Ernest Hemingway, *A Farewell to Arms*, The Hemingway Library Edition (New York:
Scribner, 1929; 2012), 216.

> ### Definition:
>
> Loneliness is "a state of lacking intimacy with the people around us."[2]

Yes, it is that. It starts internally and, like a twisty cone, swirls its way intermixed into all the other joys of life, shooting nerves into our hands so that we white-knuckle-grip any and every sign of intimacy we can find. I find myself bugging people about deadlines. Judging friends for not being closer. Judging family for not being better. Resenting relationships for not lasting longer.

I start isolating myself from criticism and indicting the world so that I can play the blameless victim of my loneliness. And many of us are certainly a victim of that insidious and crushing feeling. But where we go with the feeling — what we do with it — that can never be conflated with our lack of responsibility for having it. Otherwise, we're just handcuffing ourselves to the radiator of self-justification for the rest of our lives. What can we, the lonely, do to escape our prisons of endless isolation?

Five Aspects of Our Loneliness

Loneliness is a relational suffering, in which our buttons no longer work. Our bodies no longer give us the "feels" they once did. People no longer satisfy our souls with love as we remember it.

---

[2] Brian S. Borgman, *Feelings and Faith: Cultivating Godly Emotions in the Christian Life* (Wheaton, IL: Crossway Books, 2009), 124.

Loneliness is a predictor for all sorts of life-threatening life-conditions.[3] But we don't need decades of medical research to tell us that — *the lonely know that their loneliness will one day kill them.*[4] We have always known that our own social shortcoming would be our downfall. Installed in our fears, our operating system gives us hourly notifications:

◊ I am lost
◊ I know loss
◊ I am different
◊ I do not belong
◊ I am unwelcome
◊ I will never be known
◊ I will never be understood
◊ *I will never be able to feel okay…*

Here are five aspects of the lonely heart:

---

[3] The emerging consensus is that *felt loneliness*, rather than social isolation *per se*, is the real cause of heightened mortality rates among "the lonely." T. J. Holwerda, A. T. Beekman, D. J. Deeg, M. L. Stek, T. G. van Tilburg, P. J. Visser, B. Schmand, C. Jonker, R. A. Schrovers, "Increased Risk of Mortality Associated with Social Isolation in Older Men: Only When Feeling Lonely? Results from the Amsterdam Study of the Elderly," *Psychological Medicine* 42, no. 4 (2012): 843-53; Reiji S. Tilvis, Venla Laitala, Pirkko E. Routasalo, and Kaisu H. Pitkälä, "Suffering form Loneliness Indicates Significant Mortality Risk of Older People," *Journal of Aging Research* (2011), 1-5.

[4] Christianity is often pitted *against* loneliness, as if the two were incompatable elements of one life. But the opposite is the case. When Christ enters the picture, loneliness can expand beyond what we had previously known. For the Apostle Paul, his union with Christ heightened his longing for human-to-human interaction. "For God is my witness…that without ceasing I mention you always in my prayers, asking that somehow by God's will I may now at last succeed in coming to you. For I long to see you, that I may impart to you some spiritual gift to strengthen you—that is, that we may be mutually encouraged by each other's faith, both yours and mine" (Romans 1:9-12). "For God is my witness, how I yearn for you all with the affection of Jesus Christ." (Philippians 1:8). "As I remember your tears, I long to see you, that I may be filled with joy" (2 Timothy 1:4). The point here is simply to say that the principle that Christ is meant to fulfill our longing for (and in) human-to-human, or, "horizontal" relationships (as opposed to God-ward, "vertical" relationships) is a nice idea, but it's false, and it will mislead and oppress many who feel that they are disappointing God by longing for a spouse

It was therefore, because of Christ, even more painful for him to be apart from those he loved. Extended to marriage, Paul's experience legitimizes singleness as actually *more difficult* for Christians who are united to Christ, because they know what they do not have. They know that what they are missing out on is a picture and a manifestation of a reality that they deeply savor. This is only an example of how we can begin to use Scripture to address singleness and dating differently. It is time to cast aside the simplistic, flat use of Scripture that has riddled many books on these issues for the past twenty or thirty years. While many books have *a lot* of Bible verses, few have the hermeneutical tools to connect those verses to real life in an honest way that wins the title of "biblical."

1. A History

"I wish I was a kid again."
"I want a family."
"I want to be in love, and loved.
        Is that so much to ask?"

We are not psychopaths. We are not incapable of understanding intimacy. No, quite the opposite: *we remember*. We are there, in those moments of normal love that happened when we were children, which now haunt us with their absence. Maybe it wasn't our childhood, but our escape from childhood. Either way, we want regular intimacy, because we know that we have lost it somewhere along the way. Most people know what loneliness is because they know what love is, and they feel the awkward aloneness, not of being an individual, but of being vacated by love itself.

2. Self-Blame

"I'm alone because I can't stop
        looking at pornography."
"I deserve this emotional waterboarding."
"I'm unwanted.
        Nobody would ever want to be with a *lonely* person."

"For I know my transgressions, and my sin is ever before me" (Psalm 51:3). My obsessive preoccupation with my own sin crawls into the cracks of my loneliness, telling me the cause: *me*. You're the cause. After David sinned by sleeping with Bathsheba and killing her husband, his fixation on his own sin "seems to have possessed and overwhelmed his mind to such a degree, as to make every other consideration appear comparatively as nothing."[5] Why are you lonely? There is only one right answer. You are to blame.

---

[5] Thomas Scott, *The Holy Bible: With Explanatory Notes, Practical Observations, and Copious Marginal References* (London: C. Baldwin, 1822), 287.

3. Spiritual Warfare

"God wants you to be alone."
"He's torturing you.
            Everyone else seems happy and in love."
"You don't deserve to be with someone."
"This loneliness is inhuman.
            Maybe you should leave God,
            and try something a little more practical…"

The peanut gallery has rendered its verdict. Choose now: God, or love? Obviously, if God wanted you to be happy, *you'd be happy*. If God wanted you to be satisfied and cured of loneliness, *you would be*. But you're not. And those come in the form of voices in our head: "Many are saying of my soul, there is no salvation for him in God" (Psalm 3:2).

Our loneliness is often either caused or exacerbated by the shadow realm. Don't believe it? That's fine. A boxer doesn't have to believe he has an opponent, but he'll still withstand the brutal beating. "Your adversary the devil prowls around like a roaring lion, seeking someone to devour" (1 Peter 5:8). That's the world you and I live in, and loneliness is a favorite weapon of the skulking heavyweight.

4. Transition

"I hate this city."
"I just want to go home."
"How am I going to survive here?"

Our twenties strap us into a state that is full of turbulence, flux, vitality, versatility, but also instability. Lines are blurred. Things taken for granted in the past cannot be assumed. It is dangerous.

Our twenties are lonely because we have had all our familiarities unsettled and ripped from our hands, without anything to replace them. We face death, a new job, a new city, a new marriage, a new church — it's *all* lonely. We live in the borderlands, threatening and hostile and unclaimed and unsettled. And that is a lonely, lonely decade to live.

5. Morbid Despair

"I can't find a way out."
"I don't want to feel this way forever."
"I don't want to die alone."

That line — "I don't want to die alone" — has caused more
people to despair than almost any other thought. It will drive us to start
relationships, to fabricate emotion, to break apart families. The desire,
not merely to cure loneliness, but to avoid being utterly alone for the
next 50 years, is the weight that the lonely wake up with every single day.
"This. Forever." We feel that Jesus's curse on the abuser is already true
of us — at the bottom of the ocean, millstone around our necks,
suffocating, never dying.

God and Our Loneliness

Contrary to (justified) popular opinion, Christians are not masochists.
We are not told to love pain. On the contrary: "Persons whose curiosity
is aroused by suffering and who seem attracted by it are painfully
unhealthy."[6]

"God is teaching you something."
"God is teaching you how to be satisfied."
"God is teaching you to rejoice when it's hard!"[7]

---

[6] Andrew Purves, *The Search for Compassion* (Louisville, KY: Westminster John Knox, 1989), 86.
[7] Contrary to its common usage, 1 Peter 4:13 does *not* teach us that we must be happy *whenever* we suffer: "But rejoice insofar as you share Christ's sufferings, that you may also rejoice and be glad when his glory is revealed." Peter is not talking about suppressing chronic loneliness. Peter is not talking about pretending you're happy when you are sad. He's talking about the glory of Christ revealed through you when you are persecuted because you are a Christian — and when you are persecuted, you taste a reality more beautiful and joyful than the present suffering can counterbalance. That is why we must tread cautiously when we command real sufferers to "rejoice" — even James makes a distinction: "Is anyone among you suffering? Let him pray. Is anyone cheerful? Let him sing praise" (James 5:13). God grants power to sufferers to rejoice, yet grants them permission to lament instead.

That could possibly be true. But that doesn't nullify the fact that loneliness hurts *like somebody is vacuuming your soul out of your body through your bellybutton,* and the joy of the educational process doesn't exactly counterbalance the suffering of suffocating loneliness. Lonelienss saps us of strength. "My endurance has perished; so has my hope from the Lord" (Lamentations 3:18)

Yet, God is ... present. We all know that *presence* doesn't nullify loneliness. Fittingly, God doesn't promise to nullify it. So, we must scan our barren field for other signs of life — other signs, new gifts that the Spirit gives to our stale, disconnected souls.

1. Silence

"Okay, self: stop for a second."

Loneliness is a cacophony of dread. Its buzzing inside us is our heart digging its heels into the dirt, refusing to be drug down into silence. Silence is the greatest fear of the lonely heart: "The dead do not praise the LORD, nor do any who go down into silence" (Psalm 115:17). But silence is the rest our souls need from our overactive inputs — voices we tell ourselves, voices suggesting to us, voices accusing us, voices explaining to us.

God saves us from the silence we fear with a silence we need: "But the LORD is in his holy temple; let all the earth keep silence before him" (Habakkuk 2:20).[8] You don't have to *think* your way out of loneliness. You don't have to figure out a way to be loved. The reason the whole earth is silent before him is because he is sovereign. Read Habakkuk chapter 2: people plundering, getting drunk, shaming themselves with nakedness, cutting off people, building towns with blood and sin, worshipping idols of metal, teaching lies — all of these, embodiments of the voices that drive the lonely mad; all of these, mechanisms to forget — to avoid — the fact that we are utterly alone.

We build reputations and reels of sexual fantasies and indulge and worship, just to silence the voices that tell us we are forgotten, unknown, and unloved. And God enters our lives to silence those who seek to destroy us with our own loneliness: "Out of the mouth of babies

---

[8] And in Revelation 8:1: "When the Lamb opened the seventh seal, there was silence in heaven for about half an hour."

and infants, you have established strength because of your foes, to still the enemy and the avenger" (Psalm 8:2) — God stills our enemy-voices with those who cannot speak.

Quiet your mind. Hear the voices of your loneliness. Envision the path they would have you walk down to save yourself from that loneliness. "But the LORD is in his holy temple; let all the earth keep silence before him" (Habakkuk 2:20) The voices have been judged, and will one day fall under the wrath of God forever. Loneliness will not last forever.

2. Usefulness to Others

> "Stop looking in, start looking out.
> Can I even do that? Yes. Just do it."

Don't pretend you're happier than you are, for the sake of those suffering from loneliness like you. "Sorrow is better than laughter, for by sadness of face the heart is made glad" (Ecclesiastes 7:3). Naming our sadness is better than suppressing it. Suppressing sadness hermetically seals our loneliness from the work of Christ. And that work becomes beautiful to your neighbors who get the sense that you actually *understand* their suffering — there are few things more euphoric than *being understood.*

For lonely people, their loneliness has become "the basis of the self that they're used to."[9] You know the prayers that have been helpful for you, and those that have been unhelpful. Help others to pray words that give shape to their suffering, in ways that others may be too scared or overwhelmed to articulate for themselves. "You also must help us by prayer" (2 Cor. 1:11)

Loneliness "raises questions about God's goodness and care, and it whispers that we must have done something bad to deserve such suffering."[10] I often can't rejoice in my loneliness, but sometimes, I am enraptured by someone else's joy in pain. Take Walt Whitman, for example, who proclaims:

---

[9] Emily White, *Lonely: A Memoir* (New York: HarperCollins, 2010), 295.
[10] Ed Welch, *Side by Side: Walking with Others in Wisdom and Love* (Wheaton, IL: Crossway, 2015), 26.

"O joy of suffering! To struggle against great odds!
>   to meet enemies undaunted!
To be entirely alone with them!
>   to find how much one can stand!
To look strife, torture, prison, popular odium,
>   death, face to face!
To mount the scaffold! to advance to
>   the muzzles of guns with perfect nonchalance!"[11]

This man isn't saying something insane. "O joy to suffering!" Is this the same command that we pretend to hear — "Act as if loneliness isn't excruciating, for the glory of God." Is this suppression? No. This is expression. Whitman is caught up in the thrill of struggle. He has sort of reached his "runner's high" through his suffering. There is a small chance that we can enter into the thrill of that struggle as well — to experience loneliness as a short-term test of our own armor, clanging up against harsh and sharp realities that make us better combatants.

Loneliness could be an opportunity for reflection—space to reorder and rethink life and God. Someone who says "Stop being lonely" is a scoffer: "A scoffer seeks wisdom in vain, but knowledge is easy for a man of understanding" (Prov 14:6).[12] But a lonely person who says, "Let's rejoice" to another lonely person is a friend who sticks closer than a brother.

3. Nothing

"Let's not make this more meaningful than it is."

You may be in a very tragic place where you are — humanly speaking, perhaps you are truly alone. I feel that way 5 out of 7 days of the week. And we live in a world in which God does not fix every one of those situations. A biblically realistic approach to loneliness will acknowledge that.

---

[11] Walt Whitman, "A Song of Joys," *Leaves of Grass: A Textual Variorum of the Printed Poems, 1860-1867*, ed. Sculley Bradley, Harold W. Blodgett, Aurthur Golden, William White (New York: New York University Press, 1980), 342, stanza 145.

[12] "Whoever blesses his neighbor with a loud voice, rising early in the morning, will be counted as cursing." (Prov 27:14)

This is one of the most important things to remember when we feel lonely: we are not alone because God is punishing us, nor has God guaranteed us companionship and love in this life. We desire a Christian life that escalates from hard to easy — from circumstantially tumultuous to victorious.[13] But the Christian life (and all of life itself) remains far more tumultuous than our testimony-oriented culture would have us believe. The book of Lamentations does not end with joy. It ends with a flickering candle, hope on the verge of being destroyed: "Renew our days as of old—unless you have utterly rejected us, and you remain exceedingly angry with us" (Lam 5:21-22):

> "If I were composing this book, I would put the words of hope in God at the end. I would make them the grand finale that resolves the pain and sets light against despair. But the poems in Lamentations grow shorter, less energetic, more diminished. ... But that may be the way of healing. Hope rises up and then fades, comes and goes, as the survivors slip back into numbed despair. Hope barely survives in Lamentations. It is nearly engulfed yet not utterly silenced by the surrounding chapters."[14]

The gift that God gives us is the awareness that the universe owes us nothing. Our loneliness may be the very opportunity to learn that our suffering is both less meaningful than the ambitious would have us believe, and so much more meaningful than the culture of modern romance would have us suffer.

4. Something

> "Literally anything and everything
> is right around the corner."

---

[13] "American Christianity's a *market* form of Christianity, for the most part. It's all about identifying with a winner. That's why Easter Sunday the churches are full, but Good Friday they're empty. I'll show up when the winner pops up. But . . . don't tell me about the Saturday in which, echoing Nietzsche, God is dead, even for Christians." Cornel West, Lannan Foundation, lecture delivered in Santa Fe, NM, June 25, 2003. Quoted in Shelly Rambo, *Spirit and Trauma: A Theology of Remaining* (Louisville, KY: Westminster John Knox, 2010) 129 fn. 49.

[14] Kathleen O'Connor, "Voices Arguing About Meaning," in *Lamentations in Ancient and Contemporary Cultural Contexts*, ed. Nancy C. Lee and Carleen Mandolfo (Atlanta, GA: Society of Biblical Literature, 2008), 29 [27-31].

To the lonely, there is a sense in which God cannot and will not do anything helpful. They are trapped—isolated from intimacy. We're not sure why, but constantly frustrated in their attempts to find stable connection. But God *does* promise to be with his people — *and doing something.* When Adam was lonely in the garden, it was a God-induced loneliness that was meant to heighten his desire for a gift that God would give him: a wife.

No matter the feeling, the circumstance, the tragedy—he never leaves nor forsakes, and he is certainly never idle. A biblically realistic approach will also acknowledge that God never departs from the lonely:

> "The spine of lament is hope: not the vacuous optimism that 'things will get better,' which in the short run is usually a lie, but the deep and irrepressible conviction, in the teeth of present evidence, that God has not severed the umbilical cord that has always bound us to the Lord."[15]

God is at war for us, even as his suffering, lonely, wilderness-people:

> The eyes of the LORD are toward the righteous
> and his ears toward their cry.
> The face of the LORD is against those who do evil,
> to cut off the memory of them from the earth.
> (Psalm 34:15-16)

In reading, "The LORD is near to the brokenhearted and saves the crushed in spirit," I get a little disappointed. He saves them, does he? Remember, sister or brother in Christ: the world *will* break us in chaotic violence regardless of whether or not we have faith. But God guides us through brokenness and healing for our good. The Christian life is lived in-between:

> "He keeps all his bones;
> not one of them is broken."
> (Psalm 34:20)

---

[15] C. Clifton Black, "The Persistence of Wounds," in *Lament: Reclaiming Practices in Pulpit, Pew, and Public Square* (Louisville, KY: Westminster John Knox, 2005), 54 [47-58].

"Let me hear joy and gladness;
    let the bones that you have broken rejoice."
(Psalm 51:8)

In the context of our absolute *lack of guarantees* — other than that we will
either be broken by God or the world — God promises to protect our bones when we need protecting, to sometimes break them so that we begin to pray for joy, and to hear the cry of the righteous. Loneliness is excruciating, the birds are chirping today, the flowers are growing today, and the same God who provides for them hovers over the Siberian wasteland that you feel in your soul. Perhaps today is the day that he will sprout a seed of comfort among your broken bones.

5. The Church

"God, help me to find what
I need among your people."

Personally, church feels like the loneliest place in the world. There is no larger group of people in my proximity who are different than me than church. People have happy marriages. People belong. Ushers are ushering. People are singing. People are *singing* words you know you don't believe.

Church can sometimes make people feel even lonelier than they already are. It's understandable. But there is this part of it, where people get together every week and stay in contact throughout the week, praying for and serving one another, which God orchestrated for the communion and fellowship of his people. That seems somewhat relevant to the lonely.

"It is an inescapable feature of our human situation that we are freed or enslaved by the way others love or hate us, thus enabling us to become or preventing us from becoming the people we were created to be."[16]

---

[16] Colin E. Gunton, *The Christian Faith: An Introduction to Christian Doctrine* (Malden, MA: Blackwell, 2002), 45.

The church is *supposed* to be the place where people "Love one another with brotherly affection. Outdo one another in showing honor" (Romans 12:10). Yet, loneliness can become magnified when everything is focused on "fellowship" — stigmatizing the one who does not feel a sense of belonging.

That's fine. The church doesn't have to be the place where you feel like you belong. But it can be the place where you begin to feel comfortable in your own skin. Perhaps the gift which God intends to give you in your loneliness is not *relief* from loneliness, but the transformation of your loneliness into solitude — into the meaningful sort of self-awareness that begets creativity and meaningfulness out of the pain. I can't tell you whether your loneliness means anything. But if there is any place where mystical and spontaneous meaning occurs, it is under the preaching of the word and in the taking of the sacraments. Perhaps in your heart at the table, or in your ears under the pulpit, God will break your cocoon of unbearable emotional suffering with the razor of being comfortable with oneself.[17]

Lastly, the church can teach us that love is a process, and that loneliness is not necessarily a barrier to that process. Paul thanks God, not for perfect love, but for growing love: "We ought always to give thanks to God for you, brothers, as is right, because ... the love of every one of you for one another is increasing" (2 Thessalonians 1:3). If our sense of loneliness in this world is a product of an overly-romanticized or eroticized love, witnessing the real, slow, in-process love of sinners toward one another may teach us how to crawl out of the caves of isolation in which we feel perpetually stuck.

One final point on the church: If you feel like the church has actually made you *more lonely*, feeling *further from God* over time, then it's okay to "fast" from that. It's okay to take a break from the whole "gospel in your face every Sunday, *it's gonna be a show*, because you need this — *I'm telling you, you need this!*" type of event. You don't need that. Take a break. Find your center. Reintroduce yourself to God outside the confines of this place of terrible unbelonging. If you find belonging there, great. But if you don't, it's okay to recognize that and back away. Don't

---

[17] Anthony Storr, teaching practicioner of psychiatry at Oxford, wrote: "Modern psychotherapists, including myself, have taken as their criterion of emotional maturity the capacity of the individual to make mature relationships on equal terms. With few exceptions, psychotherapists have omitted to consider the fact that the capacity to be alone is also an aspect of emotional maturity." *Solitude: A Return to the Self* (New York: Ballantine, 1988), 18.

let the "ideal" become the enemy of the "good." Is it ideal to go to church? If it's hurting you, in a sense, it doesn't matter. Forge your own path, theological tribes and denominations be damned.

Conclusion

Real humans are lonely. You are lonely. Welcome to the human race. More than that, welcome to the sufferings of Christ himself:

> He was despised and rejected by men;
> a man of sorrows, and acquainted with grief;
> and as one from whom men hide their faces he was despised,
> and we esteemed him not.
> (Isaiah 53:3)

It doesn't feel real. But the hollow, hazy, desperate feeling you have in the chest was felt by Christ. It's felt by those around us who suffer the same way. We must learn the skill of taking it easy on ourselves for the sake of our souls — the blades that dig loneliness into our shoulders as a punishment for sin are sharpened with lies. Yet, we also must learn to be hard on ourselves for the sake of sanity. If we refuse to stop searching for intimacy — with God and neighbor — we will find it. It feels like an empty promise, but we *find* the peace that comes with meaningfulness *in the searching*.

Love is the meaning of life, and it is the fulfillment of the law. It is no wonder that its absence wreaks havoc, like barbed wire dragged through our hearts. Love's absence causes compulsions in us. It causes despair in us. It incites grief and sorrow and low self-esteem in us. Our hope is the same as Christ's — that our loneliness would bear fruit and dissolve: "Out of the anguish of his soul he shall see and be satisfied" (Isaiah 53:11). We sometimes fail to pray for release, for meaning, for realism, and for usefulness — but God has granted them to us. When we can bring ourselves to experience loneliness as meaningful and helpful to us in the short-term, we encounter a fresh way of *feeling lonely* that does not require us to despair.

As it regards God and his presence, his omnipresence can feel so generic as to fail in its pastoral relevance to our real-time loneliness, to the silt and concrete settled in our lungs. On this note, I have no eloquence to add beyond Augustine's prayer, caught as we are between knowing intimacy and longing desperately for it — a paragraph we can speak to God, and analogously those humans us with whom we long to be intimate:

> Late have I loved you, beauty so old and so new: late have I loved you. And see, you were within and I was in the external world and sought you there, and in my unlovely state I plunged into those lovely created things which you made. You were with me, and I was not with you. The lovely things kept me far from you, though if they did not have their existence in you, they had no existence at all. You called and cried out loud and shattered my deafness. You were radiant and resplendent, you put to flight my blindness. You were fragrant, and I drew in my breath and now pant after you. I tasted you, and I feel but hunger and thirst for you. You touched me, and I am set on fire to attain the peace which is yours.[18]

---

[18] Augustine, *Confessions*, Oxford World's Classics, trans. Henry Chadwick (Oxford: Oxford University Press, 1991), 201 (10.27.38).

Chapter 4
Lust

Disclaimer:
This is the worst chapter in the book.
See Addendum.

"I've been loyal to the wants of my lustful heart
And unfaithful to my friend Love."[1]
—David Ramirez

I'm tempted to write this chapter in hiding — either by wearing a mask (like a coward) or by lobbing honesty into your world like a grenade, plugging my ears in fear of judgment. I stand at the gate of sex-worship, wandering in and out, a familiar face to the demons there. In heaven, there will be people there whom I have seen and experienced, whom I should not have seen and experienced.

I have spent many nights isolated, alone, looking at pornography — some nights pushed into godly grief that produced months of repentance, and others pushed further from God into a numb haze.

I remember sitting on the edge of a bed — with a girl I loved, a girl to whom I made promises, a girl with whom I belonged to a church. We sat there next to one another, on a crumpled comforter, the edge of the mattress slightly bending underneath us. My arms were stiff, planted parallel to my torso like two table legs, holding up my slumped frame. Her back was curved forwards, arms crossed. She had a long sexual history, but I didn't. "I'm so sorry," I said. "I'm sorry." She stood up. "Now you're just like every other guy in my past." And she walked out of the room. I looked in the mirror: "Now you're just like every other guy." My worst nightmare.

---

[1] David Ramirez, "Fire of Time," *The Rooster — EP* (Sweetworld, 2013).

Why do we do this to ourselves? Our sexual desire confronts us with our most animalistic tendencies — but they hurt so much because they are also our must human tendencies. So when we experience sexual regret, and twisted sexual desire, we experience us against ourselves in the most violent terms. Lust aggressively expands, beyond our mechanisms of control, breaking our will, ridiculing our discipline. And we are left in dark rooms, on the edge of beds, apologizing for our fulfillment schemes. We are confused and unsettled about our two incompatible intuitions: that our desire for chastity is holy, and so is our desire to have sex with those around us. This tension is, at least for me, the most basic root of all my Christian hypocrisy.

We cannot speak meaningfully about sexual lust (henceforth, lust) until we have a definition:

> ## Definition:
>
> Lust is a desire for romantic intimacy with a person, which is disproportionate to the degree to which you value that person.[2]

Sex is about value (there I go … into hiding). That's why sex and money are so commonly connected — both are good things that we are tempted to experience as ends in and of themselves, unusable by God and unwantable by a true Christian. But lust isn't about value. The business of lust is to tinker with the proportions of value, so that reality feels and looks a certain way to us — certain curves, certain angles, certain scenes, certain opportunities; events made out to transform us for the better when they transform us for the worse. Lust artificially inflates the value of a certain opportunity, and depreciates others. There are five aspects of the lustful experience that help us understand what it does to us.

---

[2] This is my rephrasing of Gary Watson's helpful articulation of the complexities of sexual desire: "The strength of one's desire may not properly reflect the degree to which one values its object." Gary Watson, "Free Agency," *The Journal of Philosophy* 72 (1975) 209-210 [205-220].

Five Aspects of Our Lust

When we lust, we salivate for that experience that is worth our attention. What is it that we are really looking for when we are hungry for another person? What do we think they will give us that we find valuable?

The experience of touching
skin with skin.
A body.
A face.
A date.
An orgasm.
A cuddle.
Companionship.
To be known.
To be chosen.
To be safe.
To be loved.
Nights-not-alone.
Pictures to parade before others.
To feel, again, hopefully.
To feel desired.
To be touched.
To cry with someone.
To laugh with someone.
To be with them and only them
because there is no one like them.

Which of these do we desire more than the person themselves? Our lust is not our desire to copulate. What a sad and small perspective on sex — even on the physical act itself. Lust is not about avoiding sex, nor indulging in it. Lust is a window into the moments when lust doesn't exist — it tells us about who we are as humans, both when we are "turned on," and also when our hearts beat slowly. If we can look at lust — the out-of-proportion desire for romantic intimacy —

through the right lens, we can situate it in a way that makes more sense of our whole lives.

There are five aspects of sexual lust, defined as we have here.

1. Imitation

> "He's not my type."
> "I *need* to have her."

We learn how to want sex — big, small, smart, strong, tall, dark, handsome, blonde, brunette. Simple objects of desire. Lust is certainly intuitive enough in its hardware. But our wanting is complex machinery. And we don't learn how to want well. Similar to how we learned to speak as a child, "desire itself is a language that all men and women speak."[3] Philosophers call this concept "mimetic desire" — the idea that our sexual wanting is more than wanting something, but wanting like someone.[4]

We feel, at a level, that our lust is authentic to us. But it isn't. Lust is not original to us. I learned from my dad, from media, from friends, from boundaries I have crossed, from pornography. Desire is not spontaneous compulsion, but patterned imitation. Our desire to have sex is our impersonation of that which we are hardly aware. Our sexual preferences, even the craving itself, are inherited.

2. Topology

> "Come here."
> "Let's go to my place."

Lust is a search for a place to belong — a *topos* (i.e., "place" in Greek). Lust is a topological malfunction. Sex is as much a place as it is

---

[3] Jay Clayton, "Narrative and Theories of Desire," *Critical Inquiry* 16, no. 1 (1989), 33 [33-53].

[4] René Girard is often credited with repopularizing this concept. "Only mimetic desire can be *free*, can be *genuine* desire, human desire, because it *must* choose a model more than the object itself. Mimetic desire is what makes us human, what makes possible for us the breakout from routinely animalistic appetites, and constructs our own, albeit inevitably unstable, identities." René Girard, with Pierpaolo Antonello and João Cezar de Castro Rocha, *Evolution and Conversion: Dialogues on the Origins of Culture* (London: Continuum, 2008), 58.

an act — a place with someone. And as our lust boils up inside us, we feel our sense of place reaching dangerous instability.[5] It is at the center of the story of Israel:

> "The land for which Israel yearns and which it remembers is never unclaimed space but is always a place with Yahweh, a place well filled with memories of life with him and a promise from him and vows to him. . . . Israel is the strange people who pursued a sense of place."[6]

When we lack a place, we *roam*. We roam the internet. Our eyes roam the streets. Our imaginations roam the possible worlds, where we are gods, caught up in ecstatic pleasure. For Kierkegaard, "Boredom is a demonic pantheism. If we remain in it as such it becomes evil . . . . in the unity of boredom admiration and indifference have become indistinguishable."[7]

And boredom is a result of placelessness. Lust is topological dissolution — a disorientation of one's place.[8] When we don't have a place, our imagination invades the place of others, roving hands and faces and lips for a physical sense of "I am yours, and you are mine."

3. Mysticism

> "I can't believe I did that."
> "I couldn't stop."

Sex has always been a religious rite, because we sense the mysterious draw of "otherness" — sex is the seal of countless historic

---

[5] For example, note the instability Augustine feels when he leaves the *place* of his body: "You command me to abstain from sleeping with a girl-friend . . . . But in my memory . . . there still live images of acts which were fixed there by my sexual habit. These images attack me. While I am awake they have no force, but in sleep they not only arouse pleasure but even elicit consent, and are very like the actual act. . . . During this time of sleep surely it is not my true self, Lord my God?" Augustine, *Confessions*, Oxford World's Classics, trans. Henry Chadwick (Oxford: Oxford University Press, 1991), 201.

[6] Walter Brueggemann, *Land: Place as a Gift, Promise, and Challenge in Biblical Faith*, 2nd ed., Overtures in Biblical Theology (Minneapolis: Fortress, 2002), 5.

[7] Søren Kierkegaard, *Either/Or* (trans. Alastair Hanney; New York: Penguin, 1992), 231.

[8] "Lust thrives in privacy and isolation, and lustful people often feel shame, which also motivates them to keep their struggles hidden from others." Rebecca Konyndyk DeYoung, *Glittering Vices: A New Look at the Seven Deadly Sins* (Grand Rapids, MI: Brazos, 2009), 177

cults, and lust the source of their euphoria. It is undeniably powerful.[9]

Sex is not merely "regulatory" behavior, blowing off steam — although, it is not necessarily less than that. We have explained sex with every academic discipline that we have.[10] And yet, to fail to recognize its mystery, its being beyond us, we will lust not only with disproportion, but with pretense. We don't understand our own sexuality. It can't be categorized or explained in 5 words, or 500,000 words. In the moment of rapturous temptation, the power of our rational faculties is never more threatened, and the mysteriousness of sex is never more irrefutable.

The urge for sexual connection, and the veiled allure of that desire, while not entirely spiritual, is not entirely physical either. It is existential, expressing something fundamental about who we are that we rarely have the patience contemplate when it confronts us.

4. Guilt

"I hate myself."

"Of course I did."

"I don't know if I'm really a Christian."

We are ashamed of our lust. It is no wonder David uses such deeply physical metaphors when he slinks before God after his sexual sin: "blot out my transgressions," "wash me," "cleanse me," "in sin did my mother conceive me," "purge me," "wash me" (again), "blot out my iniquities," "create in me a clean heart." (Psalm 51:1, 2, 5, 7, 9, 10). It's a simple, roaring plea: *It's in me. Get it OUT!*" "Stop me." "I hate it." "I hate me." "Bleach me."

I am continually driven to sex in order to find the release for my pain.[11] Shakespeare walks us through the cycle of madness in the midst of temptation, which leads to guilt:

---

[9] Modern psychoanalysits admit: "Lust contains the unknown more than the known." Galit Atlas, *The Enigma of Desire: Sex, Longing, and Belonging in Psychoanalysis* (New York: Routledge, 2016), 26.

[10] See Frederick Toates, *How Sexual Desire Works: The Enigmatic Urge* (New York: Cambridge University Press, 2014).

[11] Maximus the Confessor, a 7th century church father, described the cycle of lust and pain well: "In seeking to avoid the burdensome experience of pain, we fall into the arms of sensual desire . . . , and in struggling to soothe the anguish of pain through pleasure, we only strengthen its case against us, in that we are incapable of having pleasure apart from torment and tedium." *Quaestiones ad Thalassium* 61; CCG 22, 89, 94-91, 100; PG 90, 629D–632A. Cited in Balthasar, 197–198.

The expense of spirit in a waste of shame
Is lust in action; and till action, lust
Is perjured, murderous, bloody, full of blame,
Savage, extreme, rude, cruel, not to trust,
Enjoy'd no sooner but despised straight,
Past reason hunted, and no sooner had
Past reason hated, as a swallow'd bait
On purpose laid to make the taker mad;
Mad in pursuit and in possession so;
Had, having, and in quest to have, extreme;
A bliss in proof, and proved, a very woe;
Before, a joy proposed; behind, a dream.
All this the world well knows; yet none knows well
To shun the heaven that leads men to this hell.[12]

5. Degradation

"I can't stop."
"I need more."
"I need to have relief."
"I don't care what happens."

Yes, we can be animals. But our sexuality is not as equal to our animality as we would think. It is lodged squarely in our humanity.[13] That's why lust doesn't beget sexual inability, but *human* inability: compulsive sexual behavior (CSB) is highly coordinated with depression and anxiety.[14] Why does lust beget sadness and worry? Because it ticks

---

[12] William Shakespeare, *The Oxford Shakespeare: The Complete Sonnets and Poems*, ed. Colin Burrow (New York: Oxford University Press, 2002), 639.

[13] Indulged lust creates in us "depraved notions of what it means to be human." Bruce K. Waltke, *An Old Testament Theology: An Exegetical, Canonical, and Thematic Approach* (Grand Rapids, MI: Zondervan Academic, 2007), 211.

[14] Brian L. Odlaug, Katherine Lust, Liana R. N. Schreiber, Gary Christenson, Katherine Derbyshire, Arit Harvanko, David Golden, Jon E. Grant, "Compulsive Sexual Behavior in Young Adults," *Annals of Clinical Psychiatry* 25, no. 3 (2013): 193-200. Moreover: "The emotional life of the addict parallels the proverbial roller coaster. If unable to stave off the pain with sex, the addict plunges into despair. When another sexual binge occurs after the addict has promised to stop, the addict despairs again." Patrick J. Carnes, *Don't Call It Love: Recovery From Sexual Addiction* (New York: Bantam Books, 1991), 24.

us down, like a tent post, further from the likeness of God, into the ground of the sub-human. But the lustful know this.[15]

One church father laments, sensual lust "divides the human nature into a thousand pieces, and we, who all share the same nature, mindlessly tear each other into shreds, like wild beasts."[16] And we feel it.

God and Our Inner Human

What new thing could God say to the lustful heart? "Be holy, for I am holy" (Leviticus 11:44). Yes, we are empty and corrupt and failing. But God, the creator of our sexuality, pulls the covers off of our disproportionate affections — our lusting. Despite the twisting that lust does to our souls, God speaks to us, the indulgent, the discouraged, the disproportionate, the lustful: if "nothing prospers with you . . . it is not sign, beloved, that you are not a child of God. . . . Remember that none of your trials can prove you to be a lost man."[17]

God created sex as single beam of light, whose glow seeps into every facet of our dysfunction — our beauty-mongering. And he encounters us in our dysfunction — us and him — in this single and fundamental reality: "and they shall become one flesh."

This reality is explicitly mentioned five times in Scripture, to make five points.

1. At Home In Our Own Bodies

"Therefore a man shall leave
his father and his mother
and hold fast to his wife,
and they shall become

---

[15] "Sex addicts believe that no others exist like themselves." Patrick J. Carnes, *Don't Call It Love: Recovery From Sexual Addiction* (New York: Bantam Books, 1991), 24.

[16] Maximus the Confessor, *Quaestiones ad Thalassium*, prooemium; CCG 7, 33, 269–72; *Patrologia Graeca* 90, 256B. Cited in Hans Urs von Balthasar, *Cosmic Liturgy: The Universe According to Maximus the Confessor*, 3rd ed. (San Francisco, CA: Ignatius, 1988), 197.

[17] Charles Spurgeon, "The Believer Sinking in the Mire," MTP, vol. 11 (Ages Digital Library, 1998), 361 quoted in Zack Eswine, *Spurgeon's Sorrows: Realistic Hope for those who Suffer from Depression* (Geanies House Fearn, Ross-shire, Scotland: Christian Focus Publications, 2014), 31.

one flesh."
(Genesis 2:24)

We were *made* to want to have sex. Lust feels like it's more about flesh than "the flesh." And it is. The insane guilt that we place on ourselves for the desire for sexual intimacy is inappropriate.[18] Its legitimacy is signified *by our very body parts.* God created us this way. We are not waiting salvation from sexuality. We are not praying for God to "take the desire away." No. Sexual desire, in its fulfillment and its lack of fulfillment, is the undeniable and irremovable sign that we were created for intimacy. For eye contact. For physical touch. For mutual love. For responsibility. For home-crafting. For parent-leaving. For love-making. For self-sacrificing.

God wants me to have sex. He wants you to have sex. He made you for it, among other things. He uses sexuality as a metaphor for his intimate passion for you, and for me, his people: "Go, show your love to your wife again, though she is loved by another and is an adulteress. Love her as the LORD loves the Israelites, though they turn to other gods and love the sacred raisin cakes" (Hosea 3:1).

> "The outcome of such usage is a relationship glorious in its intimacy and costly in its brokenness. The Bible understands that sexuality is the ultimate arena of cost and joy; for that reason, sexual imagery is appropriate to Israel's most treasured relationship."[19]

2. Sexual Attunement

"God, help me to do what is
sexually right in my season of life,
and not borrow from the 'me' in other seasons."

"Therefore a man shall leave

---

[18] "Denying the body denies the God who lovingly sculpted it from the earth. God is invested in our bodies." Thomas E. Reynolds, *Vulnerable Communion: A Theology of Disability and Hospitality* (Grand Rapids, MI: Brazos, 2008), 181.

[19] Walter Brueggemann, "Sexuality," *Reverberations of the Faith: A Theological Handbook of Old Testament Themes* (Louisville, KY: Westminster John Knox, 2002), 195 [190-195].

his father and his mother
and hold fast to his wife,
and the two shall become
one flesh."
(Matthew 19:5)

As sexual creatures, there are times when our eyes entice us, and
times when we are not enticed. We resonate with cravings for different
people, in different seasons of life. And in one moment, Jesus speaks to
the married, to the single who want to be married, and the single who
feel called to be single. Jesus cites Genesis 2:24 in Matthew 19:5 as an
answer to a question about divorce, and then riffs for us on the different
ways we sexually resonate. Jesus tunes that lust here to the key of
Genesis 2:24 — to the key of "the two shall become one flesh" — and
shows us what's beneath the floorboards of our fugitive desires. He
speaks to three audiences, three situations, three sexual dissatisfactions:

Pharisees: Sexual Diversity

"'So they are no longer two but one flesh.
What therefore God has joined together,
let not man separate.'

They said to him,
'Why then did Moses command one to give
a certificate of divorce and to send her away?'

He said to them,
'Because of your hardness of heart
Moses allowed you to divorce your wives,
but from the beginning it was not so.'"
(Matthew 19:6-8 ESV)

When we are committed, our disproportionate desire for
intimacy swerves from spouse to stranger. We long for the new. When
we have had our fill, won our prize, finished the chase, there comes a
sinking moment when we think: "Send her away" or "Send him away."
That was fun. Time for the next. Butterflies have not been sighted in

months. Sex drive is hovering at a 4/10. We call it "bored." We diversify our investment portfolio … why not our pleasures also? We are always texting, always following, always smiling at someone else. What if we're missing out on something better?

If we're honest, we're quite certain there is something better. We mentally step into the next room, emotionally allow ourselves to fall into the pillows of fantasizing about people other than our spouse. Sexual diversity — the time-tested cure for stagnant sexuality. Jesus calls this "hardness of heart," a deviation "from the beginning,"[20] an "allowance" because of weakness. The principle can be applied to divorce, but the *heart* of the Pharisees' inquiry was a demand to a liberated perspective on monogamy. Jesus calls it what it is: horniness multiplied, unqualified, unabridged, unfenced, lurking its spider-legs into our spouse-love.

Jesus calls the desire for sexual diversity what it is — not an "appreciation of beauty," but a scar on the face of love because of sin.

Disciples: Sexual Promiscuity

"'Whoever divorces his wife,
except for sexual immorality,
and marries another,
commits adultery.'
The disciples said to him,
'If such is the case of a man with his wife,
it is better not to marry.'"
(Matt. 19:9-10)

We want options. We want out. We want what the disciples want: "better." When God speaks with us face to face, we want to say "If." It's so easy to let our lust turn us into animals — sniffing frantically for the next morsel of pleasure, irrespective of its origin. If only we would remember the beginning, with Jesus: our own source, a torch and smoking pot, guiding our solitary physical counterpart toward us while we wait.

---

[20] "Man and woman are face to face. Here their equal rank is given even more emphasis: man looks around him and meets with an answering gaze that turns the one-who-sees into the one-who-is-seen." Hans Urs von Balthasar, "Woman as Answer," in *Creation and Humanity: The Sources of Christian Theology*, ed. Ian A. McFarland (Louisville, KY: Westminster John Knox, 2009), 150.

Eunuchs: Sexual Calling

"Not everyone can receive this saying,
but only those to whom it is given.
There are eunuchs who have been so from birth,
and there are eunuchs who have been made eunuchs by men,
and there are eunuchs who have made themselves eunuchs
for the sake of the kingdom of heaven.
Let the one who is able to receive this receive it."
(Matthew 19:11-12)

Eunuchs. Ouch. "Well, there are nights I'd rather be a eunuch than stuck in bed sexless, frustrated, tightly wound, pressure-built like a cartoon steam engine." The disciples call this "better." But we know better. We didn't ask for the calling. We didn't ask for the singleness. We are not all of us able to "receive this saying." But, for those of us who are left wanting, who are spouseless, who are "those to whom it is given" (for now), whether we want it or not, we live in a season in which chastity is our holiness; in which purity is our holiness; in which proportion-izing our desire for sexual intimacy is our holiness; in which valuing our sexually attractive neighbor more than our "sexual needs" is our holiness.[21]

God demands physical castration from none of us. But to those who are not yet married, even the betrothed, Jesus acknowledges the weight of sexlessness; of companionlessness: "Not everyone can." And that acknowledgment is a sublime relief for those who can't.[22] I know I can't. Even before the smartphone revolution, I knew I couldn't.

---

[21] "Understanding my own nature and identity and life with others ... is bound up with understanding God's nature and identity and life with others." William L. Power, "*Imago Dei — Imitatio Dei*," *International Journal for Philosophy of Religion* 42 (1997): 131-141.

[22] John Calvin helps us to know that the desire for sex is not a weakness: "If any seem more decent and modest than others, they are not, however, chaste. The sin of unchastity urges, and lurks within. Thus it is that God, by fearful examples, punishes the audacity of men, when, unmindful of their infirmity, they, against nature, affect that which has been denied to them, and despising the remedies which the Lord has placed in their hands, are confident in their ability to overcome the disease of incontinence by contumacious obstinacy." (btw: incontinence is the lack of self-control; contumacious is the stubbornly deviant behavior, and obstinacy is stubbornness). John Calvin, *Institutes of the Christian Religion*, trans. Henry Beveridge (Peabody, MA: Hendrickson, 2008), 841 (4.13.21).

God lights the runway toward harmony with those around us to whom we are sexually attracted. He pauses the moment of eye contact and says, "This is a call to put that desire in its place — *and it does have a place.*" "In sex, life is not just self-centered individuality, on the contrary, sexual desire, in its deepest meaning, is self-sacrificing."[23]

3. Sacramental Attainment

> "God, help me to see what
> the true value of sex *really is.*"
>
> "Do you not know that
> he who is joined to a prostitute
> becomes one body with her?
> For, as it is written,
>
> > 'The two will become
> > one flesh.'"
>
> But he who is joined to the Lord
> becomes one spirit with him."
> (1 Cor. 6:16-17)

It's easy to miss the point: "Don't visit prostitutes. Check." Don't allow such shallow conceptions of your own sexuality to do deep violence to your humanity. Paul is here uncovering the fragile center of our desire for sex: a desire to encounter God "face to face at the mountain, out of the midst of the fire" (Deut 5:4).

When I lustfully indulge, that indulgence requires me to forget who I am. I'm searching for a new way to be me — leaving behind an identity. I'm searching for a place to belong — for some place to offer an identity; for some person to say: "I choose *you.*" But in the moment of indulgence, I notice how I always have to put on a mask. Looking at a computer screen, looking into the eyes of the woman toward whom my intensions are not whole, I exchange my sincere self for a sly smile: a fig

---

[23] Leon R. Kass, "Appreciating The Phenomenon of Life," *Hastings Center Report*, vol. 25 (Special Issue, 1995), 7.

leaf of a look, if there ever was one.

Lust is never the lowest common denominator of our desire for sex. God has traded his sparse mountaintop meetings with prophets for an indwelling of our very bodies. Our union with Christ "is not merely a reminiscence of or a reflection on Christ's benefits but a most intimate bonding with Christ himself."[24] God lifts the veil, and uncovers what we rarely admit sits at the taproot of both our love and our lust — of our proper desiring and our disproportionate desiring — Christ himself, in us, emanating and claiming value (positive or negative) over our every sexual act.

4. Meaningful Sex

"I don't just want pleasure.
I want life-giving pleasure."

"Because of your hardness of heart
he wrote you this commandment.
But from the beginning of creation,

'God made them male and female.'
'Therefore a man shall leave
his father and mother
and hold fast to his wife,
and the two shall become one flesh.'

So they are no longer two but one flesh."
(Mark 10:5-9 ESV)

The text in Mark 10 is nearly identical to Matthew 19 — they recount the same event, followed by Jesus's encounter of children and a teaching about wealth. But Mark has a different emphasis. Mark zooms in on Jesus's interaction with the Pharisees. No disciples. No eunuchs.

Two differences are relevant for us: (1) In contrast to Matthew, Mark records Jesus's citation of Genesis 1:27: "he made them male and female" (Mark 10:6); (2) When Jesus ministers to children immediately

---

[24] Herman Bavinck, *Reformed Dogmatics, Volume 4: Holy Spirit, Church, and New Creation*, trans. John Vriend, ed. John Bolt (Grand Rapids, MI: Baker Academic, 2008), 567.

after his teaching on marriage, he was not only "laying his hands on them," but he *blessed them*" (Mark 10:16).

Jesus's reflection — "they are no longer two but one flesh" — is starkly located between "he made them man and female" and "[he] blessed them [the children]." The creational need of male and female for one another is the foundation of the sexual embrace, and children are the fruit of godly sexual embrace.[25] Mark showcases Jesus's speech to those who desire sex: Sex, in its most perfect form, *communicates safety* to the weaker party — both in its relationship, and its results. The meaning of sex is to *create a safe place for the weak to be loved* — it is what Christ does for us in our union with him.

Physical touch by the more powerful party is always meant to be a blessing of protection. Calvin comments: "For the law was made solely for the protection of the women, that they might not suffer any disgrace."[26] Whenever someone who is more powerful touches someone less powerful — whether it is sexual between spouses, or non-sexual between adult and child — that touch of the powerful party is intended to be one that is both protective and blessing. God created sex as both an occasion to experience and express safety, as well as a cause for weak vessels to enter the world who can experience that same safety. "In sensual pleasure, the human spirit seeks a self-centered substitute for giving itself to God; this alternate gift of self thus isolates the person in his egoism, rather than uniting him with the beloved."[27] "One flesh" *means* "I will protect your body as my own. And I will protect our children as I would protect my own body."

"And he took them in his arms and blessed them" (Mark 10:16). It is no coincidence that casual sex is often the occasion for abandonment (of the sexual partner and the child): the lust which caused the initial contact is fully expressed in its violence toward the act's creation. Sex performed without the intent to communicate safety will express itself in full disdain when it is called upon to play a protective function that was never part of the original act.

---

[25] This is, of course, not to say that those struggling with infertility are *less* in any way. And yet, the very reason infertility is so painful is because it points to the greater reality which compels us to care, to protect, to adopt, to *be parents*. At the end of the day, in God's economy, the desire to copulate and the desire to co-parent are variations one and the same holy desire.

[26] John Calvin, *Commentary on a Harmony of the Evangelists, Matthew, Mark, and Luke, Vol. 2*, trans. William Pringle (Edinburgh: The Calvin Translation Society, 1845), 381.

[27] Hans Urs von Balthasar, *Cosmic Liturgy*, 3rd ed. (San Francisco, CA: Ignatius, 2003), 196.

Sex is meant to be a *critique* and *healing* of coercion and the utilization of the human body. The *meaning* of sex is safety; the purpose of sex is the depiction of Christ's love for me, and for you. And lust in its disproportionate value on the self over the other, like a forest fire, burns down the boundaries that make sex the opportunity of peace for the weak — even for ourselves.

5. The Reconciliation of the Animal and the Spiritual

"God, help me to know what it means
to say 'Yes' and to say 'No.'"

"Therefore a man shall leave
his father and mother
and hold fast to his wife,
and the two shall become
one flesh."
(Eph 5:31)

When we behold someone's sexual possibility for us, we feel the tension in our existence between our animal pieces and our spiritual pieces, ripping us in different directions. Augustine makes the undeniable point that we feel, never more than in a moment of lust, that God "created man's nature as a kind of mean between angels and beasts."[28] We are caught between using someone and worshipping them. We tell ourselves that we don't want to use the person; no, we adore them, and would do anything to be with them. "I love you so much. I'd do anything for you." A common branch of latent and suppressed sexual lust. That's why worshipping another person is not *valuing* them. When John worships the angel, the angel deflects.[29]

And so, we arrive at a reality that feels undoable for us: There is no higher way to value a human being than to regard their relationship with God as your highest priority. In a moment of lust, such desires seem irrelevant and trivial. "Sanctify her." "Cleanse her." "Present her full

---

[28] St. Augustine, *City of God*, 12.2(1).

[29] "Then I fell down at his feet to worship him, but he said to me, 'You must not do that! I am a fellow servant with you and your brothers who hold to the testimony of Jesus. Worship God.' For the testimony of Jesus is the spirit of prophecy." (Rev 19:10)

of splendor." "No one ever hated his own flesh, but nourishes it" (Eph 5:29). It's no surprise that these feel like sexual nonessentials — they are *difficult* and *laborious* tasks; certainly not a "turn on" (...we think). Why does the spiritual aspect of our sexuality always feel like a wet blanket for the animal aspect, when we explain it? Acting out on our lusts is one of the easiest things we will ever do on this earth. And valuing someone else's relationship with God — who is able to satiate what we often consider our greatest and least spiritual desire — is one of the most uphill decisions we will ever make. That's why Paul says of our being "one flesh" with someone: "This mystery is profound, and I am saying that it refers to Christ and the church" (Eph 5:32).

Lust closes the gap of that mystery by narrowing our vision. That's why lust does such a disservice to our sexual desire. Lust presumes to entirely depict the sexual act, yet never fails to isolate rather than fulfill the user. Why? Because the mystical aspect of sex rejects us when we quantify it insufficiently. Our "distrust arises from our measuring the thing itself by the narrowness of our own understanding."[30]

Conclusion

For the desires of the flesh are against the Spirit,
and the desires of the Spirit are against the flesh,
for these are opposed to each other,
to keep you from doing the things you want to do.
But if you are led by the Spirit,
you are not under the law.
(Galatians 5:17-18)

We can never judge ourselves for pursuing a physical fulfillment to our physical desire. Christians love explaining the spirituality of sex — its origin and meaning — but to neglect the physical is to impoverish the spiritual. The "rational soul" isn't mean to be at the reigns 24/7. The basic purpose of our sexual desire as human beings is to pursue its

---

[30] John Calvin, *Commentary on Philippians*, tr. T.H.K. Parker (Edinburgh: The Saint Andrews Press, 1965), 283.

fulfillment. A holier person might say, "No, it's to serve as a metaphor of our desire for God." No. The purpose of our hunger for food is not to fast — it's to eat. And the purpose of our sexual appetite is to be fulfilled. And since that fulfillment has its proper place and context, the stronger the desire, the stronger we will pursue that proper place and context.

Do we ever fulfill it improperly? I don't know any adult who hasn't. Sexual desire, in God's plan, joins the physical and the spiritual. It does not require us to neuter our "sex drive" with spiritual meditations. Nor does it require us to compromise the spiritual integrity which makes our desires meaningful. God gives us a metaphor and a goal which is both the "before" and the "after" of our every sexual urge. Those who are united to Christ do not have less sexual desire than those who have Christ. Nor do we necessarily have "better" sex. But we do have a person who explains our sexual desire, toward which we aspire, in which we understand ourselves, and within which we are neither a victim nor a master of our own selves.

We will *always* feel the tug of lust. It will always pull at our souls, nagging us, telling us to give in, telling us to despair, reasoning with us until our minds are tired and our bodies are eager. God will not fully redeem you until you are fully in his presence. "The desires of the Spirit are against the flesh, for they are opposed to each other, to keep you from doing the things you want to do." (Galatians 5:17)

Yes. "*Things.*" So many "things." And so much time left not to do them. That is the call and the condition of the Christian life. And it is neither a cause for a cry of victory or despair, but of resolve to run the race which is laid before us.

This is my least favorite chapter in this book, because we both know that in this season, no Christian writer can be fully, publicly honest about their experience of lust and maintain their platform. Until then, we have to trod our path between our public and private selves, at least until the public becomes a place where Christians can write honestly about their experience without the threat of exile. All we can do is try to find the humanity in the sexual desire — to find the goodness in our sexual longings and not judge them because of their strength or their object.

Lust is always a twisting of a good thing. Christian purity culture has created an industry out of throwing the proverbial baby out with the bath water — suppressing God-given desire for sex in the name of "fighting sin." God never requires us to choose between being a human and being a Christian, despite what evangelical culture may communicate in practice. May God give us mercy to find the intimacy that we were created to experience without the Puritanical misgivings of those who help us in so many other ways.

Addendum:

I'm not sure if I ever "came out of hiding" in this chapter. There is so much shame here. So many "institutional higher-ups" with axe-in-hand. So many wolves waiting to devour the weak. This chapter was written through my "Evangelical" avatar, in some ways.

I'm not sure if we will ever have a culture where we can speak openly about sexuality. Especially about lust, singleness, and twenty-something-ness. I hope that one day such a space exists — supplying safety to those with something to say.

Currently no such place exists in arm's reach of Evangelicalism. So, we tack in our veiled honesty with footnotes about and bible texts. Sanitized. Unashamed, but unprocessed — and so secretly shamed, but publicly accepted. Each one of us left to our own secrets.

Chapter 5
Anxiety

"Let us express our envy
for the man with a steady job
and no worry about the future."[1]
—Ezra Pound

I'm scared to death of conservative Christian men. *"But you're a conservative Christian man!"* Yes. Relatively speaking, I suppose that's true. But that makes my anxiety all the more impractical — like an arachnophobic tarantula. But I have this little emotional twitch. I'm always waiting for that phone call from … someone; anyone: "Just give up, Paul. Go home. We found out that you're a fraud."

I've received that call before. And I've seen every structure in my life, which I took for granted, dissolve before my eyes because of that phone call. A half-story about my sin spread like wildfire from person to person. I had no control over what people thought I did. I had no control over how I was perceived. And I didn't even know who was spreading the rumors.

For the first twenty-five years of my life, the only thing I was scared of was spiders. Now it's spiders and conservative Christian men. I'm hypervigilant around them. Walking into a seminary class feels more like walking into a lion's den than anything else. I used to walk into meetings as the leader — chest out, confident, belonging. Now, I have an overactive "spidey-sense" always tapping me on the shoulder: "Run." "He's out to get you." "You can't trust him." "They all think you're pathetic." "They *see you* for who you are. They will reject you."

---

[1] Ezra Pound, *"From* Lustra I, III" in *The Poetry Anthology, 1912-2002: Ninety Years of America's Most Distinguished Verse Magazine,* The Modern Poetry Association, ed. Joseph Parisi and Stephen Young (Chicago: Ivan R. Dee, 2002), 7-8.

Twentysomethings tend to accumulate "triggers" from one experience or another. Everybody's is a little different. But it becomes the nerve in which anxiety digs its claws. Anxiety can take us from enjoying a beautiful day with our friends or family, to spilling our guts all over the floor with no idea why we're bludgeoning ourselves and loved ones so brashly.

Anxiety comes from the Greek word ἄγχω (*ángcho*), a verb which means, "I compress, press tight, especially the throat; I strangle, throttle, choke." It's possible to experience anxiety as a sound — an unbearable, high-pitched beep, squeal, or pop. It makes sense, in the scuffle of murderously clawing into an unwanted future— the infinite future packed neatly into a little bombshell, waiting to blow shrapnel into your stomach the moment you arrive.

Whether it's the punishment in an hour, or the lunch tomorrow, or the contract renewal next year, or the worsening health of your parent … the future is always tapping you on the shoulder, letting you know that all your flinches won't stop its right to make you squeal. Anxiety is a wraith, flopping over the marshlands of our circumstances, commanding us to fear, commanding us to surrender, looking for *us*. Our definition of anxiety fits the picture.

Definition:

Anxiety is "the emotion of serious distress,
which is aroused by impending danger, evil, or pain,
whether real or imagined."[2]

---

[2] Brian S. Borgman, *Feelings and Faith: Cultivating Godly Emotions in the Christian Life*. (Wheaton, IL: Crossway Books, 2009), 124.

Five Aspects of Anxiety

"Fear" is too pedestrian and homiletical — "we have nothing to fear but fear itself." It's too familiar to seduce us into confronting what really terrifies us — that is, all our silent hypotheticals. I am not merely afraid. I am silently *scared* — silent even to my own mind. 99% of the time, my anxiety is a secret I keep from myself — one that I feel, but don't speak. Built into the engine of anxiety is avoidance, and that avoidance pushes our anxiety deeper and deeper into our bodies, below the brain stem, into our guts and chests. The hypotheticals of public shame revolve in my head like a mobile over a crib — spinning me downward into a hypnotic state of alertness: cringing, waiting, anticipating the pain, the loss, the tragedy.

1. Pain

"It will happen again."
"You live in a world where *that* happens *to you*."
"You can't endure it ... not after what they did to you."

I'm still waiting for that phone call: "Just stop. Just please stop trying, and go home. You are not Christian enough to be doing what you're doing."[3] That's why I don't answer numbers I don't know. That's why I don't check my mail. That's why I don't trust people. I want to foresee the damage. I want a chance to flinch. We are a flinching people, the anxious. Just give us a chance to squeeze our eyelids together as tight as we can before you burn our world to the ground.

"One of the characteristics of acute suffering is its tendency to obliterate all other experience. It can become almost impossible to see, hear, or feel anything beyond one's own suffering, as though that suffering were all that existed in the world."[4]

---

[3] My whole story feels like living in Maroth: "The inhabitants of Maroth wait anxiously for good, because disaster has come down from the LORD to the gate of Jerusalem" (Micah 1:12) — waiting anxiously for good, but anticipating further disaster whose source is God alone.

[4] Carol A. Newsom, "Book of Job," *The New Interpreter's Bible*, vol. 4 (Nashville: Abingdon, 1996), 520.

2. A Threat

"You are on your own."
"Don't trust them. They don't understand."
"Run. Retreat. Jab. Withdraw."

The anxious feel the true threat that constantly surrounds them. Even if God exists, we cannot suppress the commonsense notion that the world is impartial and cruel. "God's reign is proclaimed as a present reality, but it is always experienced
by the faithful amid opposition."[5] Anxiety tells us something about the universe: that it is dangerous. Anxiety comes in voices. When we are afraid, we outsource our interpretation of reality to those voices, latched deep within our brains like little aliens with a control panel.[6]
And we obey the voices we hear — the false prophets. We heed the whispers of the "insiders," who have the skinny on the world that none of your normal friends have. We acquiesce to the threats they tell us. Whatever is true of the world, it is threatening. And whatever is true of God's love, the world is still full of malice that appears totally divorced from his care.
Our hearts are prophets, telling us about the future — but what sort of prophets are they?

---

[5] J. Clinton McCann, "The Book of Psalms," in *The New Interpreter's Bible: Old Testament Survey* (Nashville, KY: Abingdon, 2005), 212.
[6] There is a theory in psychology called "Attachment Theory," and it depicts one's internal psychology voices, which psychologists call "managers." The louder, bossier managers are called "firefighters" — they sit at our "conference table," and operate on the presumption that they decide who sits at the conference table, and not us. To the degree that we recognize: *we* decide who is invited and who is not — which voice is welcome, and which is not — these voices speak with equal power, but less authority. See Pehr Granqvist and Jane R. Dickie, "Attachment and Spiritual development in Childhood and Adolescence," in *The Handbook of Spiritual Development in Childhood and Adolescence*, ed. Eugene C. Roehlkapartain, Pamela Ebstyne King, Linda Wagener, Peter L. Benson (Thousand Oaks, CA: Sage, 2006), 197-210.

"In the Old Testament, prophets were the ones who talked about the future, and much like worriers, what they foretold was often bad. The only way you could remain in good standing as a prophet was if your predictions were infallible. Err once and you were forever banned from making future prophecies (Deut. 18:22). Using this standard, worriers are certifiable false prophets."[7]

Regardless, they speak to us. And they speak persuasively.

3. Apocalypse

"If you lose him, life won't be worth living."
"If you miss out, everyone will know you're pathetic."
"If you don't make the cut, your future is over."

This is more than "The sky is falling."[8] To the fearful heart, every moment that it makes contact with the world is a possible apocalypse — a potential ending of the world and everything that is lovely in it. Instead of electrons and protons, the world is composed of impending doom. Full stop.

"I looked at the earth—and there, a formless waste:
    to the heavens—and their light was gone.
I looked at the mountains—and there, they were quaking;
    All the hills were trembling.
I looked—and there, no human beings were left;
    All the birds in the heavens had fled.
I looked—and there, the garden land was desert
    And all its cities had been pulled down,

---

[7] Edward T. Welch, *Running Scared: Fear, Worry, and the God of Rest.* (Greensboro: New Growth Press, 2007), 52.

[8] Academic psychologists call this "catastrophizing" (and popularly it has spawned the term "awfulizing") — imagining the worst possible scenario, and then judging that possibility the end of the world. Catastrophizing is higher among males than females, and catastrophizers experience pain more severely than those who value mental toughness and optimism. See Edmund Keogh and Gordon J. G. Asmundson, "Negative Affectivity, Catastrophizing, and Anxiety Sensitivity," *Understanding and Treating Fear of Pain*, ed. Gordon J. G. Asmundson, Johan W. S. Vlaeyen, and Geert Crombez (New York: Oxford University Press, 2004), 91-116.

Before Yhwh, before his angry burning. (Jer 4:23-26) [9]

The anxious heart feels all of these words — formless, quaking, trembling, fleeing, pulling down, deserted, dark. Yes, God threatens to make these words true of all Israel. The anxious heart experiences Jeremiah 4 as true of the entire galaxy.

4. Overthinking

"What if she finds out?"
"What if I never get married?"
"What if I ruin everything?"

Anxiety leads us down a billion hypothetical paths, and all of them are universes populated by every single person except the God of Scripture. We think faster than we can feel, leaving our emotions racing to keep up with the prophets predicting doom to hail down all around us at any moment.[10] "Even though I walk through the valley of the shadow of death, I will fear no evil, for you are with me; your rod and your staff, they comfort me" (Psalm 23:4). Yeah. No rod, no staff, no "you," and certainly no comfort — but there is plenty of evil. And there is plenty of chaos.

Shall we stack up another Bible verse against experience to see how it holds up? "In God I trust; I shall not be afraid. What can man do to me?" (Psalm 56:11) Well, let's brainstorm. Man can humiliate, disfigure, abandon, torture, kill my loved ones … anything else

---

[9] John Goldingay, *Old Testament Theology, Vol. 3: Israel's Life* (Downers Grove, IL: IVP Academic, 2009), 803-804. For Kierkegaard, "The nothing around which anxiety forms itself is usually the future. Inasmuch as the future is fraught with possibility, our relationship to the future is fraught with anxiety." Gordon D. Marino, "Anxiety in the Concept of Anxiety," in *The Cambridge Companion to Kierkegaard*, ed. Alastair Hannay and Gordon D. Marino. (San Francisco, California: Cambridge University Press, 1998), 319.
[10] Anxiety causes further exploration of emotions — "You need to pay attention to this." And thus, depression begets a cycle of reflection and introspection, further and further, looking for relevant evidence. And thus, our depressive state becomes not only the source, but the result of a chronic paranoia about our destitute circumstances, reading all data as evidence of loss and hopelessness. Depression can be the spark that burns down a soul's stock of positive emotion under the guise of honesty. Depression is really a storytelling virus that we catch in our souls that shapes our minds, our brains, and our spirits. See Isabelle Blanchette et al, "The Influence of Affect on Higher Level Cognition: A Review of Research on Interpretation, Judgment, Decision Making and Reasoning," *Cognition & Emotion* 24, no. 4 (2010): 561-595 (587).

necessary?

Anxiety feasts on those possibilities day and night, and when those thoughts are not in the fore of the anxious heart, they are the white noise behind everything else. Anxiety, like a chameleon, can transition from being a voice in your ears to a tint of your eyes — a hue of reality itself. Anxiety blinds us, not with a blindfold, but with its own filter — highlighting harsh lights and darkening unpleasant lines of our lives until we forget that there was anything beautiful to begin with.

5. Attack

"Can you just talk to her, please?"
"Can you just come over?"
"Can you just answer?"
"Can you just *please*…?"

Anxiety causes us to *act* scared. We deploy our defense mechanisms against those who are defending us from ourselves. When we are fearful, we attack those whom we love. We nip at their souls for nourishment. Like cement, we harden and the boundaries of our souls become rigid and unstable. Our cement hearts grip tightly onto the hands of others — "You're hurting me" — we can't hear it above the ringing. "I *need* you." We are scared, so we latch onto others and hold them accountable for our fears. We attack because we are afraid.

We feel the squeeze of loneliness compound the uncomfortable heat of anxiety, so we require of others what we cannot offer ourselves: resolve. We ignore our internal resources. We resign ourselves over to our fears. And we operate on the assumption that we can do nothing for ourselves. The attention of our loved ones, because they are so willing, is often the very first addiction created within the anxious heart.[11]

---

[11] Anxiety can be quiet, too. Anxiety, our silent puppeteer — "Jump!" "Worry!" "Blame!" "Despair!" — our strings are invisible to us, but our actions toward others remain mysterious until we admit that we are afraid.

God and Our Anxiety

When I was a kid, I had terrible nightmares — about losing my family and about monsters. My mother comforted me when I would wake up screaming. I'd cry with the relief of reality, feeling a love strong enough to expel the terror.

As an adult, nights are different. Now, I struggle to sleep — not because of nightmares, but because life itself has become the nightmare. As we grow older, monsters trade their closing shifts for first shifts. We're greeted by our fears, not as nocturnal anxieties, but as waking worries.

Dreams can still be scary, but reality is straight terrifying. That's why people drink at night while they watch Netflix. That's why people jump on their favorite app — Instagram, Minecraft, or Facebook — when they're waiting on bad news. That's why we check our phone for texts first thing in the morning. That's why the Psalmist cries, "In the night my hand is stretched out without wearying; my soul refuses to be comforted" (Psalm 77:2). Our triggered indulgences are simply our childlike riffs on weary hand-stretching at dusk — our soul's variations on refusing the realities of the dawn.

Is there a word for it — reality-phobia? Our worries are the same, but more specific than when we were children — and now they bully us with "You *really can* lose it all."

The suffering of a family member shakes us with our powerlessness, and our failure to fix them. Failure at work ties our hands to the plow with the rope of "If you fail, you are *a failure.*" The four words "I have a lump" are strong and violent enough to shatter our brittle lives like glass.

Lord, don't let us complicate this with self-help. Don't let us throw plastic life hacks at the iron-cold situations which touch our deepest God-wanting. Grant us comfort in the midst of the nightmare reality can sometimes be, when waking up is not an option. Even better, wake us up with your "perfect love" that "drives out fear" (1 John 4:18). Turn our eyes to what we know, when our heads, our bodies, and our emotions refuse to accept your place in our fears.

Screwtape writes, "There is nothing like suspense and anxiety for barricading a human's mind against the Enemy. He wants men to be concerned with what they do; our business is to keep them thinking about what will happen to them."[12] Okay, Screwtape. Game on. Here are a few things "The Enemy" enables his people to say:

1. Sin-Awareness

"My anxiety may have alterable components."

God makes us aware of our own sinfulness. This is irritating and unfitting truth that the anxious heart does not want to hear. A result of our sinfulness, "Instead of trust and intimacy, fear and anxiety reign in the human sphere."[13]

Our own sinfulness is not comforting. But *knowing* that we are inclined from birth to be people-using, God-forgetting, and self-serving shows us that we are actually in the boxing ring with ourselves. "The heart is deceitful above all things, and desperately wicked" (Jeremiah 17:9).

Knowing our own sinfulness places a wedge between our hearts and our minds — between our anxiety and our inner thoughts. "I am the kind of person whose heart lies to itself." It's the difference between being hypnotized and being in an armbar — "Why are you cast down, O my soul, and why are you in turmoil within me?" (Psalm 42:5).

God licenses us to prosecute our voices, as well as the judgments they insist about us, with the gavel of Jesus Christ: "Hope in God; for I shall again praise him, my salvation" (Psalm 42:5). Maybe not right away. Your emotions probably won't listen to your commands. They may even win that battle. In fact, in the midst of this very Psalm, David *loses* to his fear. He commands his emotions, "Hope in God" in verse 5. And then he immediately follows up with, "My soul is cast down within me" (Psalm 42:6). He lost.

So, *he repeats himself to himself* in verse 11: "Why are you cast down, O my soul, and why are you in turmoil within me? Hope in God; for I shall again praise him, my salvation and my God." Not all will come

---

[12] C.S. Lewis, *The Screwtape Letters* (New York, NY: Macmillan, 1961), chapter 6.
[13] Waltke, *An Old Testament Theology: An exegetical, Canonical, and Thematic Approach* (Grand Rapids, MI: Zondervan, 2007), 309.

to destruction tomorrow. The truth of total depravity empowers us to demote our besetting anxieties from the place of "mind-controller" to "opponent." Now you know that you can go to war with them. Now they are conspicuous. Now they are conquerable.

2. Circumstantial Change

"I may be rightly worried."

The common advice, "Anxiety is not *really* about your circumstances, but your heart" is true, but not *absolutely* true. Scripture is replete with godly anxiety that is dependent on circumstances. David prays:

> But I am like a deaf man; I do not hear,
>> like a mute man who does not open his mouth.
> I have become like a man who does not hear,
>> and in whose mouth are no rebukes.
> (Psalm 38:13-14)

> But for you, O LORD, do I wait;
>> it is you, O Lord my God, who will answer.
> (Psalm 38:15)

David is not merely trying to get his head right. The burden is not *on him* to completely eradicate his heart of anxiety. What is the solution to "I do not hear" and "I am … a mute man?" The answer is: "It is you, O Lord my God, who will answer." David finds himself unable to speak against voices. He finds himself stuck in his anxiety, powerless before the voices of accusers and the circumstantial doom which his suffering speaks over him, and God does not place on him the burden of repenting his way out of it.[14]

And Paul, in his letter to the Philippians, in which he tells them "do not be *anxious* about anything" (Phil. 4:6), also expresses his wish to send his friend Epaphroditus to Philipi "that you may rejoice at seeing

---

[14] John Goldingay comments, "The psalm contains no plea for forgiveness in light of its admission of sin, only a plea for God not to rebuke and chastise (as God has been doing), not to abandon and be far off but to hasten to deliver." John Goldingay, *Old Testament Theology, Vol. 3: Israel's Life* (Downers Grove, IL: IVP Academic, 2009), 290.

him again, and *that I may be less anxious*" (Phil. 2:28).[15]

Will God directly solve all of our circumstantial problems if we invite him with enough positive supplication? No. But the opposite isn't true either. God *really does* act on our behalf and changes our circumstances and answers our prayers with a "Yes" *sometimes*. It's not unspiritual or sinful to be anxious about circumstances. God does not require us to *always* make anxiety a "heart issue" which we can change by vigorously willing ourselves to be healed. Rather, anxiety is human, and it is often the mechanism that God works change in us through our circumstances.

3. Peace

"It doesn't all rest on me."

I think other Christians are better than me. They trust God, so they're blessed with peace. They pray, so God gives them that special feeling of trust that it will all work out. They sin less than me, so God gives them more. And all of this is based on a gospel that is offered to me, but is made real in my life by my own cheery go-getter sanctification — not a gospel that is offered to me, and is made real in my life by God's gracious sovereignty. But that's backwards. If I have access to peace, it is not because I am one of the lucky few who has figured out how to apply God's grace to myself — it's because it pleased God to *do it* on my behalf.[16]

Peace isn't the opposite of anxiety. Peace is *who* God is, and God shepherds the serene and the anxious — "Peace I leave with you; my peace I give to you. Not as the world gives do I give to you. Let not your hearts be troubled, neither let them be afraid" (John 14:27). This notion of "not allowing" our hearts to do something seems pivotal for encountering God's peace — "let not your hearts be troubled" (John 14:1). Peace is the result of wrestling through anxiety over time, kicking the sharp jaws of anxiety in at least four ways:

---

[15] Moisés Silva comments: "Paul, who was already bearing some heavy burdens, must have anguished over the possibility that Epaphroditus's work of mercy might turn into a new source of grief." Moisés Silva, *Philippians*, Baker Exegetical Commentary (Grand Rapids, MI: Baker Academic, 2005), 139.

[16] "For it is God who works in you, both to will and to work for his good pleasure" (Philippians 2:13).

- *Anxiety is about control.* All our hand-wringing and working and self-exhausting leads us to one place at night. What does God give to those he loves? A promise. Whether we eat or not,
  - "It is in vain that you rise up early and go late to rest, eating the bread of anxious toil; for he gives to his beloved sleep" (Psalm 127:2).
- *Anxiety is about power.* We think that the cure to all worry is the confidence that we can muscle our way out of any situation, that we can leverage our clout to shame our anxious voices. But we will never be able to muscle our way to the perfect security that God promises:
  - "His divine power has granted to us all things that pertain to life and godliness, through the knowledge of him who called us to his own glory and excellence" (2 Peter 1:3).
- *Anxiety is about waiting.* Will God do anything? Perhaps, if we do the strongest possible thing we can do — wait — God will be God for us in a way that is fresh to our fears.
  - "Say to those who have an anxious heart, 'Be strong; fear not! Behold, your God will come with vengeance, with the recompense of God. He will come and save you.'" (Isaiah 35:4).
- Anxiety is about the future. But God, in turn, does not address the whole future. In fact, he guarantees the long term will be hard. But he will nourish you today. Peace is not a result of securing the future, but being connected to something that gives you life and bliss: God himself. Apparently, God genuinely responds to trust. Anxiety feels like the rest of the world plugged itself into your socket for energy. You don't have to be that person. You don't have to be the savior of your world. Your reach is not the measure of your responsibility.
  - "Blessed is the man who trusts in the LORD, whose trust is the LORD. He is like a tree planted by water, that sends out its roots by the stream, and does not fear when heat comes, for its leaves remain green, and is not anxious in the year of drought, for it does not cease to bear fruit" (Jeremiah 17:8).

No molecule in the universe floats left or right except by God's perfect dictation. No demon enters our dreams except by his eternal decree. No threat poses itself to us except by his fatherly intention. "See what kind of love the Father has given to us, that we should be called children of God; and so we are" (1 John 3:1).

We are children who don't even understand our own trembling. We are children who would place our fears before the Father if we weren't curled up in a ball in the corner. We are children who would hear God's comforting promises, except for our cries to the world for help.

"Fear not, for I am with you; be not dismayed, for I am your God; I will strengthen you, I will help you, I will uphold you with my righteous right hand" (Isaiah 41:10).

4. Short-Sightedness

"If I keep worrying five
years ahead of today,
I will go crazy."

I am almost tired of the idea that God makes our suffering meaningful — so tired, that it has stopped being true for my heart. Suffering is not like success. Suffering is not awesome. Sometimes, I feel like God expects me to hold my scraped hands and knees before him, and flash a Stepford smile — "Thank you!" — while he pours gospel-hydrogen-peroxide on my raw inhibitions. Is that the best thing God provides for our fears — a *reason* not to scream?

But God gives more than knowledge to us, and issues more than commands toward us. God holds us in our terrors. He works helpfully without ceasing when we scream helplessly without relief. He embraces when we shiver in fear at the unknown — or worse, the known. "He meant to pass by them, but when they saw him walking on the sea they thought it was a ghost, and cried out, for they all saw him and were terrified. But immediately he spoke to them and said, 'Take heart; it is I. Do not be afraid'" (Mark 6:49–50).

The book of Proverbs counters the fear of others by saying, "The fear of man lays a snare but whoever trusts in the Lord is safe." (Prov 29:25). God's grace is for the moment when God seems like a sadistic mastermind, and we need to see that he is the one who will break the very laws of physics to embrace us in our anxiety.

5. Union

"God, walk through the darkness with me."

Anxiety *feels* like the most rational position, because all naysayers will fall under your dismissive criteria for privileged optimism — "Easy for you to say."

"Simon, Simon, behold, Satan demanded to have you, that he might sift you like wheat, but I have prayed for you that your faith may not fail. And when you have turned again, strengthen your brothers" (Luke 22:31–32). Your current situation is on the table in this tug-of-war: between the demands of Satan against the prayers of Jesus. God doesn't dissolve our fears with the promise of a happy ending. He declaws our fears with the promise of Jesus's perfectly effective prayers for you to have the strength to begin again when tragedy strikes.

God doesn't promise us that everything is going to be okay. He doesn't look under our bed and tell us that there are no monsters. He does not tuck us into the sheets of our hearts that want to be pandered to and pampered. God tells us the worst and the best.

Do not fear what you are about to suffer. Behold, the devil is about to throw some of you into prison, that you may be tested, and for ten days you will have tribulation. Be faithful unto death, and I will give you the crown of life. He who has an ear, let him hear what the Spirit says to the churches. The one who conquers will not be hurt by the second death.[17]

Not what I want to hear. I want, "Do not be afraid. You won't suffer." I want, "Behold, the devil will never harm you, because I keep watch over you." I want, "Be faithful, and I will keep watch so that your terrors never come true." If that was God's message, Jesus Christ would be irrelevant to us. If God promises that our horrors are never true, then our horrors cannot be counted as suffering with Christ.

---

[17] "Do not fear what you are about to suffer. Behold, the devil is about to throw some of you into prison, that you may be tested, and for ten days you will have tribulation. Be faithful unto death, and I will give you the crown of life. He who has an ear, let him hear what the Spirit says to the churches. The one who conquers will not be hurt by the second death" (Revelation 2:10-11).

When Daniel sees God, he doesn't get peaceful — he gets anxious: "I saw in the night visions ... one like a son of man, and he came to the Ancient of Days ...As for me, Daniel, my spirit within me was anxious." (Daniel 7:15)

Our terrors are a participation in the sufferings of Christ (1 Peter 4:13).[18] Our moments of overwhelming anxiety are our walking hand-in-hand with Jesus in the Garden of Gethsemane — Satan's house-of-horrors made specifically for Christ — which Christ endured specifically for us, so that we would endure specifically because of him.

Jesus said to his disciples, "My soul is very sorrowful, even to death; remain here, and watch with me" (Matthew 26:38) When we are afraid, we find ourselves in the midst of that invitation, flailing and crying and bleeding and agonizing over the future with Christ, so that his confident perseverance in the face of fearful and certain death becomes our own.[19]

Conclusion

"Therefore I tell you, do not be anxious about your life, what you will eat or what you will drink, nor about your body, what you will put on. Is not life more than food, and the body more than clothing?" (Matthew 6:25) That verse is either wonderfully liberating or painfully unhelpful. "Don't be anxious?" Right.

But God is so bold in this command, either because he's an unsympathetic moral dictator, or because he wants to look anxiety in its serpentine eyes a day at a time: "But seek first the kingdom of God and his righteousness, and all these things will be added to you. Therefore do not be anxious about tomorrow, for tomorrow will be anxious for itself. Sufficient for the day is its own trouble" (Matthew 6:33-34). Tomorrow will be anxious about itself. That doesn't mean tomorrow isn't scary. That doesn't mean God gets angry at us when we get scared, or that Jesus gets disappointed when our heart rate rises. Leave that brand of

---

[18] "But rejoice insofar as you share Christ's sufferings, that you may also rejoice and be glad when his glory is revealed" (1 Peter 4:13).

[19] "This was according to the eternal purpose that he has realized in Christ Jesus our Lord, in whom we have boldness and access with confidence through our faith in him" (Ephesians 3:11-12).

Christianity for the people who invented it.

Try this when you are in private:

Turn off your music, take off your headphones.
Relax your shoulders.
Adjust your feet so they are flat on the ground.
Hone in on a few sounds of the room.
      The heater.
      The birds outside the window.
      The house settling.
Breath in through your nose.
Linger in your inhale for a moment.
Breathe out through a wide open mouth.
      (Say the sound of "H" until you have no air left)
Linger in your exhale for a moment.

Breathe in again.
This is called "square breathing."

Linger Inhale
(4 Seconds)

Breathe In
(4 Seconds)

Breathe Out
(4 Seconds)

Linger Exhale
(4 Seconds)

```
┌─────────────────────────────────────────┐
│            Linger Inhale                  │
│            (4 Seconds)                     │
│                                           │
│                                           │
│  B                              B         │
│  r                              r         │
│  e                              e         │
│  a e                          a e         │
│  t c                          t c         │
│  h o                          h o         │
│  e n                          e n         │
│    d                            d         │
│  I s                          O s         │
│  n                            u           │
│  ( )                          t )         │
│  4                            (           │
│                               4           │
│                                           │
│            Linger Exhale                  │
│            (4 Seconds)                     │
└─────────────────────────────────────────┘
```

Try tracing your finger along
each side of the square for 4 seconds,
performing the task assigned to each side.

Try another square breath.
Don't "hold" your breath tightly at the top or bottom.
Just breathe in. Hover at the top. Exhale. Hover at the bottom.

This gesture will feel empty.
That's fine.
Allow your anxiety to speak.
Hear what it has to say, fully, without resisting it.

And then …
  Take the plunge back into fighting fear.
Command your soul with David.
Give your internal "tomorrow" a boot,
  with Jesus, just for a moment.
Assert yourself over your soul.
Command yourself (even if you don't listen) again and again.

That is our unique battle in life as anxious people — striking at our hypertension again and again, held hostage by anxiety's switchblade named "What If…" Parry the blade. Dig Fight back. The battle with anxiety is a pride fight — fight on this principle: Nobody tells you what to do but you.

And then …
Relax your shoulders.

It is an ebb and flow.
Rest, and fight.
Rest, and fight.
Regroup, and attack.
Seek first the kingdom of God,
  and God will be fighting with you,
  along with all of his anxieties
  and the anxieties of David

and the anxieties of Daniel
and the anxieties of Paul.

Everything is going to be okay.
You come from a heritage of worrying believers.
You are going to be okay.

You have absolutely *zero* circumstantial guarantees.
And you are going to be okay.

"Take thought.
I have weathered the storm.
I have beaten out my exile."[20]

---

[20] Ezra Pound, "*From* Lustra (1917)," 7-8.

Chapter 6
Dissatisfaction

Often I have received better than I deserved.
Often my fairest hopes have rested on bad mistakes.
I am an ignorant pilgrim, crossing a dark valley.
—Wendell Berry[1]

"I hate my life." I say it to myself all the time. I say it to my mom sometimes. I really hate it. It's great — good school, good family, enough money, all my problems are first world problems. But that doesn't change the fact that every day of my life, I wake up wishing I was someone else. Wishing I wasn't single. Wishing I didn't have to date. Wishing I was 2 years further on in my life, making 6 figures a year, in a daily rhythm of deep intimacy with God and profound self-understanding. But I'm not. Not at all. Not with singleness. Not with the dating game. Not with God — I don't think I ever remember being this far from him; and I don't know if I know how to get back.

I want to go to Europe. I want to date someone beautiful who's desperately in love with me. I want to have great abs. I want to have cute kids with my beautiful spouse in a roomy New England cottage with vaulted ceilings overlooking the Hudson River that I got on a steal. I want a job that's either 1) profoundly meaningful (i.e., poet, author, speaker, exotic food critic, or possibly a Princess Diaries situation), or 2) exceptionally exciting (i.e., Jack Bauer, Olympian, etc.).

Or maybe… maybe I would be satisfied simply with not working at Starbucks, quitting, working at Barnes & Noble, quitting, working at a publishing house, quitting, accepting a scholarship, losing it, starting a relationship, ruining it. Yes, that's basically what I'm looking for—not my life. I don't need the $150,000 annual salary or the vaulted ceilings. I

[1] Wendell Berry, *Jayber Crow: A Novel* (Washington, D.C.: Counterpoint, 2000), 133.

just need to not have this hourly-wage 9–5 that's *stealing* my prime years. I need to discover a way to dream again, because I'm dissatisfied.

Five Aspects of Our Dissatisfaction

Dissatisfaction runs my depression into the ground every night, and puppets my anxiety every morning — plucking my strings, dancing my limbs, with callous unconcern. Our definition of dissatisfaction is this:

> ## Definition:
>
> *Dissatisfaction is the relentless inability to take pleasure in life.*

Yes. Ceaseless in its dulling. Deafening us to pleasure. Burning our tongues, singing our eyes, leaving us with only a bland and blurry experience of daily life. And this fire that disappears our enjoyment, our satisfaction, it has several sources within our own souls.

1. Expectations

"It wasn't supposed to be this way."
"Nobody told me hard work wasn't worth it."
"I'm less and less happy every day…"

Growing up, people sold us on life. And we believed. We dreamed. And yet. On the other side of all that hard work: an empty apartment and a bottle of antidepressants. Oh yeah, and you have to cook for yourself now. We expected more than this from life. We expected a Rory Gilmore life — Yale, romance, poetry, partying, journalism; or some degree of that.[2] Now, we are no longer rewarded simply for showing up. "Your future" was always a beautiful and daring challenge — an opportunity to escape the monotony of our boring roots. What was marvelous has turned into a millstone. And we begin to see our parents in the mirror — in our own skin; our own eyes.

2. Materialism

"Why can't I have a job (or hair) like hers?"
"My phone, my car, my house is literally the worst."
"One day, when I have a better life,
      I'll be satisfied."

Right now, we are too tangled and busy to do anything fun, or meaningful — at least let us have *one of those*. No, every crevice of our lives now reeks of responsibility.[3] We just want enough. Enough to breathe. To coast. I didn't order this. *This is not my order*. Send it back to the kitchen. I want the American Dream.[4] And at the very least, I want to know that I'm *on track* for that dream. I have certain check boxes that need to be filled — spouse, sex, house, children, job, and happiness.[5] No, it's not as trivial as a box. It's life. Because these boxes are life.

3. Aimlessness

"Don't leave me hollow."
"I'm tired of feeling low;

---

[2] "Professors do not compare their houses or cars with those of hedge fund managers. But when hedge fund managers get ever more opulent houses and more high-performance cars, their new acquisitions change the standards of what's desirable among those on the next rung of the economic ladder." Thomas Gilovich and Lee Ross, *The Wisest One in the Room: How to Harness Psychology's Most Powerful Insights* (London: Oneworld, 2016), 191.

[3] "Yeah, I'm responsible now, the price you pay for being successful." Lando Calrissian, *Star Wars: Episode V — The Empire Strikes Back* (Lucasfilm, 1980).

[4] "The real problem is that any American dream is finally to incomplete a vessel to contain longings that elude human expression or comprehension. We never reach the Coast we think we see. . .." Jim Cullen, *The American Dream: A Short History of an Idea That Shaped a Nation* (New York: Oxford University Press, 2004), 182.

[5] "The idealized images of romantic partners in entertainment and advertising can make a date, or a life, with an admirable but not-extraordinary person seem a disappointment rather than a privilege." Gregg Easterbrook, *The Progress Paradox: How Life Gets Better While People Feel Worse* (New York: Random House, 2004), 180.

of feeling hollow."
"School is expensive; jobs are hard to get."
"No — no real passion for anything in particular."

I certainly appear aimless. I think when I get married I will be even more aimless, not less. I have seen it in the eyes of dozens of my friends in their twenties: searching, frantically, "What is my passion?" "What am I good at?" Social media allows us to be amateurs at everything and excellent at nothing. Instead of being excellent at one or two things we are neophytes to the interests of our culture. But there is a song about *motivation* that is simply not found in some souls. And that is terrifying for a world built on the thrill of one-upmanship.

The aimless feel like incompetent little sheep dressed up like wolves, hoping their teeth are sharp enough to "level up." We live in the midst of an entrepreneurial swell — "scaling" is the preferred methods of personal growth: moving a small business to a bigger business. Is there any more important process in life — in church-ing, in parenting, in dating, in working? Aimlessness is doubly dangerous, in that it can both leave us simmering in a stagnant, low-frequency malcontent, or it can push us into superficial self-improvement techniques that are driven by someone else's goal, and puts money in someone else's pocket. The aimless are scared that they have not yet found their home in any task.

Aimlessness *is* scary. We're supposed to have found that one thing that fulfills us — that one activity that brings us life. Trying things is scary because … well, what if you waste time on something and it wasn't *it*? So, why try anything when you don't know for sure if it's *the thing*? Aimlessness is an ugly cousin of perfectionism. What's a summa cum laude graduate to do when she has no motivation deeper than the 4.0? It's the same question we ask thirty years down the road in a different form: "What's a successful workaholic to do when he has no deeper motivation than the paycheck?"[6]

4. Failure

"Life just sucks.
"Trust me, I've tried already."

---

[6] I'm very thankful to Jamie K for this point.

"There is no bright side."

Face in the mud. Hearing "No" *again*. Pushing, yanking ferociously
against every hatch that leads to a better place — a fulfilling place. That's
a fast enough swell to drag us into the open waters of dissatisfaction. It's
enough to drive a man to do desperate, *desperate* things (but certainly
we're not yet there).

5. Monotony

"I need *something* to change."
"I feel stuck, shackled."
"It will be another year until I'm free.
    I don't know if I can handle it."

Ugh. Will it ever end? One after the next. And nobody
understands. No eye looks at your life and sees the sickness of it. The
repetition, like a hypnotic spiral, dizzying, blurring together, is extending
your life-time and racing through it at the same time. Is it 2019 already?
Is it 2020 already? Is it 2029 already? The questions asked by the
monotonous. The dissatisfied can't stand it. For them, time inches
slowly forward. They can't wait until the Spring, to hear back from the
admissions office; until the Fall, to apply; until the next year, when
there's an opening. Monotony is the dissatisfied heart's cold gaze at the
clock of time — tick tock: "Your meaningless life is going to change as
fast as its been changing (not at all)."

God and Our Disappointment With Life

I suppose this is where you expect us to stare down a familiar
road: "*God is most glorified in us when we are most satisfied in him.*"[7] Yes.
We are going to stare down that road. Satisfaction, our elusive friend —

---

[7] John Piper, *Desiring God: Meditations of a Christian Hedonist* (Colorado Springs, CO:
Multnomah, 1986, 2011), 10.

make eye contact with us. Facing down real-life dissatisfaction with spiritual satisfaction … did we bring a knife to a gun fight?[8]

Satisfaction *is* a gift that God gives to us. And, like a knife, the grace of Jesus Christ's satisfaction takes skill to utilize in the midst of dissatisfaction. There are five paths of satisfaction that reach each of us, in our different forms of having lost our fulfillment.

1. Pleasure

"God loves pleasure.
Maybe I should give it another shot.
A better shot."

"The righteous has enough to satisfy his appetite, but the belly of the wicked suffers want" (Proverbs 13:25). I suffer want. The Lord cares, and knows. "When my spirit faints within me, you know my way! In the path where I walk they have hidden a trap for me." (Psalm 142:3). God's path is never in a vacuum — he sees the "trap layers" around us: the million contingencies that could destroy us and render us sad and dissatisfied forever. He knows. "You know." If only we knew what God's path was for us; directions found scribbled on a Post-It in heaven. "With long life I will satisfy him and show him my salvation." (Psalm 91:16)

Even Paul's great claims about the skill of contentment come in the context of distress. Notice how he skates back and forth between speaking of his real contentment, as well as his genuine distress in Philippians 4:10-14:

Joy: "I rejoiced in the Lord greatly that now at length you have revived your concern for me.

Distress: You were indeed concerned for me, but you had no opportunity.

---

[8] There is no doubt that our intuitive conception of the *weakness* of spiritual affections is our unthinking capitulation to secular materialism: "Consumerism appears to have become part and parcel of the very fabric of modern life. . . . And the parallel with religion is not an accidental one. Consumerism is ubiquitous and ephemeral. It is arguably *the* religion of the late twentieth century." Steven Miles, *Consumerism—As a Way of Life* (Thousand Oaks, CA: Sage, 1998), 1.

Joy: Not that I am speaking of being in need, for I have learned in whatever situation I am to be content. I know how to be brought low, and I know how to abound. In any and every circumstance, *I have learned the secret* of facing plenty and hunger, abundance and need. I can do all things through him who strengthens me.

Distress: Yet it was kind of you to share my trouble." (Philippians 4:10-14)

He strengthens me with satisfaction. We are always in-between earthly dissatisfaction and the nearly imperceptible beauty of God's pleasure for us. Paul notes that it is a secret — it is a skill: to delight in God, whose grace is often too strong for our insatiable palates. Grace then, like the cross, is an acquired taste.[9] But when we learn delight, we learn to be satisfied — not as sadists, but as saints, who know that appetite is a poor guide on the path of lasting pleasure.

2. Profession

"What I feel begins with what I profess (whether it feels like it or not)."

We sink our teeth, either into tedium or transition, hoping to savor a pleasure that will *keep us*. But we find, like so many of the pleasures we seek, that we keep on spoiling. We want liberation from the tyranny of our expectations, but the only course of escaping we ever take is *to fulfill them*. That's like trying to murder your way out of the prison system — you've got a small chance of success, and a high chance of ending up there longer.[10]

---

[9] "As long as the individual perceives that pattern of consistent goodness, life may seem good overall even if nothing strongly good ever happens." Roy F. Baumeister, Ellen Bratslavsky, Catrin Finkenhauer, and Kathleen D. Vohs, "Bad Is Stronger Than Good," *Review of General Psychology* 5, no. 4 (2001): 361 [323-370].

[10] "An *expectation* is defined as 'an eager anticipation for something to happen.' A *goal* is defined as 'a purpose or objective.' When we are clinging to expectations, we are waiting for something to happen and giving our power away. As we start to identify and release our expectations, we can take more empowering steps toward achieving our goals, with a clear sense of purpose." Christine Hassler, *Expectation Hangover: Overcoming Disappointment in Work, Love, and Life* (Novato, CA: New World Library, 2014), viii.

So, we are stuck in our place — stuck to choose between learning the skill of prison-breaking, or cage-living. It is in our twenties that we choose whether to become women and men *who make professions* — not building a career, but building a life that *says something we want it to say*. I have failed miserably at this, as I've run from city to city, job to job, whole life to whole new life, searching for a place to belong. Restlessness. It can pulverize and purify our promises. Commitments carry a shrill sting: "Will I hate this?" "I do hate this." Do we leave the job? Do we leave the relationship? Do we take the risk? Life feels more like flapping in the wind than finding our path. We certainly feel entitled to a path.

> "So teach us to number our days
> > that we may get a heart of wisdom.
> Return, O LORD! How long?
> > Have pity on your servants!
> Satisfy us in the morning with your steadfast love,
> > that we may rejoice and be glad all our days."
> > (Psalm 90:12-14)

If Hollywood were to make a movie out of your life, what would be its title? What would be the character arc? What themes would you trace? How would it end? We get another day — that's our "long life." What does it mean to "number our days?" It means: "Count today. One. You have it. And there will come a day when God counts 'zero.'"

We defined dissatisfaction at the beginning of the chapter as "the relentless inability to take pleasure in life." Let's define satisfaction as living and enjoying a life "one could, when delivering their eulogies, reasonably deem 'good.'"[11]

All of our lives profess something. Conviction is the seedbed of all our expectations. Live a profession you believe in. In finding a conviction — whether it is a cause, a person, a creative endeavor, a pressing issue, the building of a family — you may find a way forward in the midst of your dissatisfaction. "If you pour yourself out for the hungry and satisfy the desire of the afflicted, then shall your light rise in the darkness and your gloom be as the noonday" (Isaiah 58:10). What need

---

[11] Daniel M. Haybron, *Happiness: A Very Short Introduction*, Very Short Introductions (New York: Oxford University Press, 2013), 41.

can you fill in the world, rooted in God's love for it? Maybe it's just in your family, or your church, or your community — but find it. What is the "desire of the afflicted" for which God has given you limited days to pour yourself out? When you find it, and pursue it, "then shall ... your gloom be as noonday."

3. Production

"If I start to *try*,
satisfaction will start to bloom."

"I made great works; I built houses and planted vineyards. . . . I made myself gardens and parks, and planted in the all kinds of fruit trees. . . . I bought male and female slaves. . . . I also had great possessions of herds and flocks. . . . I also gathered for myself silver and gold and the treasure of kings. . . . I got singers . . . and delights of the flesh, and many concubines. So I became great and surpassed all who were before me in Jerusalem." (Ecc. 2:4-5, 9)

The author was lost, and will be lost. One hundred years before him, he was not a thought. One hundred years later, dilapidation had taken him. Another notch in the belt of the universe; and yet, his life meant something. Our dissatisfaction is our constant reminder that life is more meaningful than we will ever be able to grasp — that the purpose of our seeking and building and acquiring and learning and dating and stockpiling is deeper still than all those activities.[12] It's not instagrammable. It's not a cabin in the woods. It's not a trip to Europe. Our striving for more is the inextricable sign of our humanity. Our dissatisfaction pushes us up, up, pressing us further than we have the strength to go; compelling us beyond our settlings and shortcomings, if

---

[12] Robert Wuthnow insightfully comments: "Protestant writings about work, money, and materialism . . . [show] a legacy of concern about overwork, greed, possessiveness, and other sins of the flesh in these writings, but ... there is also a great deal of accommodation in them to the secular spirit of our age." Robert Wuthnow, "*Introduction*: A Good Life and a Society: The Debate over Materialism," *Rethinking Materialism: Perspectives on the Spiritual Dimension of Economic Behavior*, ed. Robert Wuthnow (Grand Rapids, MI: Eerdmans, 1995), 19-20 [1-24] Cf. Marsha G. Witten, "'Where Your Treasure Is': Popular Evangelical Views of Work, Money, and Materialism," *Rethinking Materialism: Perspectives on the Spiritual Dimension of Economic Behavior*, ed. Robert Wuthnow (Grand Rapids, MI: Eerdmans, 1995), 117-144.

we were only satisfied.[13]

> "The eye is not satisfied with seeing,
> or the ear filled with hearing."
> (Ecclesiastes 1:8)

4. Purpose

> "I must have a sense of purpose.
> I will not despair.
> It's right around the corner."

Our purpose can completely change the meaning of our situation. That's why we're 15 minutes late to work, and *exactly right on time* on a first date. "What's in it for me?" Ecclesiastes tells us: "All the toil of man is for his mouth, yet his appetite is not satisfied. . . . Better is the sight of the eyes than the wandering of the appetite: this also is vanity and a striving after wind" (Ecclesiastes 6:7, 9). Save me from feasting on a banquet in the grave: "Those who once feasted on delicacies perish in the streets" (Lamentations 4:5).

We've got plans for fulfillment. *Oh, we've got plans.* But God's got plans on plans on plans. God knows an *end* for our ends. That line might preach from a pulpit, but can we feel it when we face our demons of dissatisfaction? Like food and sex and accomplishment and meaningfulness, all of which are justified by their purpose of pleasure, God has a purpose for us — even in our aimlessness.[14] In our stumbling addiction to "leveling up" and life-hacks, between psychotic motivation and stagnancy, God insists that there is still a deeper purpose: to relieve us from "such weariness as no amount of sleep could ever dispel."[15]

Our dissatisfaction is the thread which God wove within us — a reminder: "You branches were meant to widen and spread and bud. This

---

[13] "Beginning is going on. Everywhere. Amidst all the endings, so rarely ripe or ready." Catherine Keller, *Face of the Deep: A Theology of Becoming* (New York: Routledge, 2003), 3.

[14] Aimlessness can serve as a real-time prompt for us to trust God: "Guaranteed security dulls the memory. Guaranteed satiation erodes the capacity ... to be open to how it might yet be." Walter Brueggemann, *Land: Place as Gift, Promise, and Challenge in Biblical Faith*, 2nd ed, Overtures in Biblical Theology (Minneapolis, MN: Fortress, 2002), 51.

[15] Hans Urs von Balthasar, *The Heart of the World*, trans. Erasmo Leiva (San Francisco: Ignatius, 1979), 152.

place may not have space for that." Dissatisfaction pushes us to investigate our sense of purpose sufficiently to know: "Should I stay, or go?"

Dissatisfaction is a constant reminder that we have a longing that will never be fulfilled in this life — a purpose which will never fully reach its end until our last day. This is a hard pill to swallow, partially because we don't have a palate for grace. It's not intuitive, but we can take delight in the daily reminder that nothing satisfied in this world because *our desires* we wont' settle for anything less than the purpose for which they were created: a right relationship with God. Satisfaction begins to come, to land on the tongue, to become tasteful and satisfying *as we go*. We elsewhere say that delight is a skill. Likewise, *grace* is an acquired taste. And it culminates in the reality that, like enjoying some caviar or foreign mushroom dish, *savoring* God's culinary skill applied to our joy is an end in and of itself — a perfect circle of satiation that comes naturally to none of us.

5. Praise

> "God, be the beginning and ending
> of all my satisfaction."

God gives himself: "Delight yourself in the LORD, and he will give you the desires of your heart" (Psalm 37:4). Yes, we *know* this. Psalm 37:4 feels like we're pitting spiritual fulfillment against spiritual satisfaction. But be patient with the verse. David digs deeper into the center of this notion elsewhere: "The LORD is my shepherd; I shall not want." (Psalm 23:1)

Oh. "I shall not want?" But I *do* want. "He makes me lie down in green pastures. He leads me besides still waters." Hmm. In our best moments, those are very wantable things. Not when we see our old friends getting six figure jobs. Not when we see all our friends getting married and having babies while we struggle to get a date and have kids of our own (not on the same day). Not when we haven't eaten all day in an insane cycle of crash dieting. Not when we're alone with our smartphone on a Friday night. But the "me" who is broken beneath all our misdirected impulses *desires* the green pastures, the still waters. "He leads me beside still waters. He restores my soul. He leads me in paths of righteousness for his name's sake." (Psalm 23:2-3).

Okay. I get it now. God doesn't pit our desire for him against the desires of the world. He makes our desires sane and better.[16] "For I will satisfy the weary soul, and every languishing soul I will replenish" (Jeremiah 31:25). He washes, dries, and irons our day-old wants, and gives them back to us fresh. God doesn't take the apple away from us. He trades our McDonald's Apple Pie for a fresh, organic apple ripe from the wild. He trades our thousand-volts, bloodshot, surging compulsions for a
sustainable sense of existence.

There was a season in college when I was *really* into lifting weights. I would go to the college gym every day with the same guys — grunting, pushing, hoo-rah-ing, flexing. For years, my "max" bench press weight was such an easy way to quantify my masculinity, my success, my value as a human being. I saw others who didn't follow this system of measurement as less, as unambitious, as settling for a lesser life. I felt caught up in a beautiful tension of dissatisfaction, because *satisfaction* was so quantifiable and attainable: just lift, and eat, and work hard, and you will be satisfied. I hypnotized younger guys into this cult, convincing them that love and appreciation and longing awaited them on the other side of the weight room. I could see the light spark up in their eyes as I told them about this gospel, this ladder, this pathway to joy and life and satisfaction.

Years later, the "bench press gospel" still beckons my name: "There is real joy here, you know." There was a season where I was walking closely with an NFL lineman who could bench press over 500 pounds. And he was very much as dissatisfied as I was. But that doesn't dissuade me from believing that I could be happy, if only I could attain a six pack, and a muscular back, and fame and fortune from it all. Yes, that sounds quite reasonable. Or, perhaps it's death in a "life" costume. And the only radar which can see the death woven into the "bench press gospel," which will save young men from using steroids and save young

---

[16] Nicholas Wolterstorff comments, "Human insatiability proper is not a function of animality, however, but of spirituality. . . . The human mouth can be satisfied—for the time being at least. But the human eye and ear are insatiable, forever eager to see and hear something new (as well as often wishing to revisit the old)." Nicholas Wolterstorff, "In the Cage of Vanities: Christian Faith and the Dynamics of Economic Progress," *Rethinking Materialism: Perspectives on the Spiritual Dimension of Economic Behavior*, ed. Robert Wuthnow (Grand Rapids, MI: Eerdmans, 1995), 173 [169-192].

women from the anorexic "size zero gospel" is God himself. We can fight it, and heal, and escape from these false promises of satisfaction, but only with other false promises.

We still face "death" and "enemies" and "evil," but the *God* variable qualitatively changes all of that: "For you are with me." Sorry, what does that have to do with my dissatisfaction? "Whoever has ears to hear, let him hear" (Matt 11:15). We may find peace in this world. We may find comfort and contentment. But so far as we render God irrelevant, green pastures and still waters will evade us. Our enjoyment of God is the purpose and pure form of all our other enjoyments. The giver is the gift, and so long as we miss that, we'll be a kid under a Christmas tree who shows love for the sake of the Playstation. All our earthly satisfactions are from God, and they are for us— and both of those realities need each other, "according to his good pleasure, which he purposed in Christ" (Ephesians 1:9).[17]

Conclusion

We're not simply dissatisfied because we want to be wealthy and prestigious. Dissatisfaction is *simply* our way of existing in the world as it is — broken and hurting. Our churches don't satisfy us. Our friendships don't satisfy us. Our relationship with God is harder than we thought it would be, *and yet* our dissatisfaction is explained by many unsatisfying truths. And will inform our hearts when we are dissatisfied. There is a great reconciling to be had between our expectations and the reality of God's working — we will *only* be satisfied in Him, and this creates all sorts of holy and unholy dissatisfactions of sinning saints who are works-in-progress.

Our greatest satisfaction is coming: we will "fall down before him who is seated on the throne and worship him who lives forever and ever" (Rev. 4:10) — before the one who is dissatisfied with sin and satisfies us with his love.

---

[17] Wolterstorff, again: "Since we are not naked souls, our bodies in the end always triumph over any attempts at completely spurning materiality . . . . But since we are not merely animal beings, our spirits always rebel against being confined to the world of pure nature." Wolterstorff, "In the Cage of Vanities," 186.

Part of this life will be the stark disappointment of knowing we get glimpses and tastes — divine pleasure is almost like a dream in that way: it is able to plumb the depths of our affections in the deepest sense, but it is not fully manifest in our real world. "You open your hand; you satisfy the desire of every living thing." (Psalm 145:16)

Satisfy us, God, with the satisfaction in you that we have forgotten. And help us to receive our earthly satisfaction as gifts from you; faint peeks into the throne room, dropped on our tongues in the Lord's Supper, in the jazz riff, in the romance, in the family, in the job security, and in our loss of them all. Help us to experience the impossible, but the real: that you are enough.

Chapter 7
Self-Hatred

"Don't you on the whole
regret that I am Walt Whitman?"
      —Walt Whitman[1]

I'm *not* a "southern boy." Not at all. I'm from Hyde Park, New York. I wear a Yankees hat. I attended a private, heavily Jewish day school growing up. I'm *not* a southern boy. And yet, I found myself sitting in the cab of my pickup truck in Dallas — naturally, it was for a girl. I'd moved there — with the best intentions — in a bad season of life. I was looking for stability. I was hoping to find belonging, acceptance, normality, from a woman, from a place. I was looking for somebody who would make me feel "okay." There were moments of ecstasy. I think I had experiences in Dallas that felt more like heaven than anything I've ever felt ever in my life.

And yet, moments like this one, right after a screaming fight, sitting in my car, I was repeating to myself over and over again, in different intonations and tones: "You're a piece of s***." Over and over again, for probably an hour. She didn't say anything accusatory. It wasn't her fault. I was simply lost in the Phantom Zone of my own consciousness, imprisoned. I couldn't have stopped repeating my unholy mantra to myself if I wanted to. Some would have me dragged away to a hospital somewhere. But self-haters know: we exist on this plane 24 hours a day. Self-hatred is not like self-blame, like swallowing some terrible medicine. No. Self-hatred is more like emotional anorexia — it's a fundamental psychic reality that never leaves; it stalks us always, when

---

[1] Basil De Selincourt, *Walt Whitman: A Critical Study* (New York: Mitchell Kennerley, 1914), 188.

it isn't assaulting us.

When I wake up, as easily as yawning, I bathe my soul in self-disgust. When I turn to God, to my Bible, and to Christian blogs, I feel that disgust sanctified as the condition for grace. I imagine God with a golden sticker, eagerly anticipating my confession: "I'm worthless and terrible and stupid and inconvenient." He
responds with a heavy smile, "Now that you have admitted it again, I can give you the gospel's cure. See you tomorrow." Like a lost and lowly Oliver looking for grace, "Please sir, may I have some more?"

I operate under a clear impression that God would prefer me with a healthy dose of habitual self-disgust. If I admit I am not allowed to give grace to myself, *then* I can have some. My weak attempts to assure myself "You're okay" feel like I'm stealing from God's cookie jar of grace. I often get the sense that the concept of self-love is unwelcome in Christianity, and incompatible with the good news of Jesus Christ. It feels like a regular ritual of self-deprecation is the precondition for our receiving grace. And that spins out into all sorts of negative self-talk elsewhere in our lives.

My accomplishments, *they don't matter.*
My failures, *they just show who I really am.*
My friends, *they feel bad for me.*
Compliments I receive, *they're just pity.*
My addictions, *no one can know.*
My addictions, *they're the only thing that*
                  consistently makes me happy.
My reputation, *people think I'm pathetic.*
My body, *it's okay … in the right mirror, with good lighting.*
              No, it's disgusting.
My spouse, *"Please don't leave me."*
"I love you." "…thank you so much for loving me."

I can't remember a time when I *really* liked myself — like, how I imagine Bradley Cooper probably likes himself. I think I could have matched that level of self-satisfaction when I was six or seven. We hate ourselves with the wrath and the respect of a thousand middle school bullies, and with the skill and sophistication of a trained CIA torturer.

We judge and reject our emotions, our dispositions, our dreams, our trajectories, with dozens of voices collected from our past — friends, parents, bosses, bullies, and lovers. When we try to think positive thoughts, we only lock eyes with our snickering inner torturer: "Happiness? That's a silly thought."

This hate surfaces in a million different ways. We rehearse scripts of self-loathing to ourselves each day. We defer to bending our expandable souls to the whims of others in relationships, twisting us into a more crooked posture every time. We apologize for being ourselves. We go to the gym seven times a week. We hate a friend because they are better than us. We fear saying the wrong thing and making someone mad. We binge. And purge. And purge. And purge. In moments of silence, my mind goes into autopilot: *Stupid! Stupid! Stupid!*

We live flinching lives. Don't spill that pasta sauce. Don't be too needy. Don't be fat. Don't be annoying. Don't be wrong. Don't be stupid. Don't be awkward. Don't be a fool. Don't want too much (or too little). Don't, don't, don't — because as soon as you use up your strikes, you might as well pack up your things in this world and move on, because your chances at being loved — at being worthy — they're over. See ya. Gone.

Five Aspects of Our Self-Hatred

That's enough waxing eloquent on self-hatred. We need a working definition.

> ## Definition:
>
> *Self-hatred is the habitual feeling of disgust toward oneself.*

Self-hatred is a singular repulsion planted within your self-talk which feels completely natural and justified.

If there is any chance of escaping the deafening ring of endless self-hatred, we need to zoom in on our inclinations. My self-hatred is too common and credentialed to dismiss in one swipe. I need to know where the inception occurred. I need to know its grooves that stamp my soul "Unacceptable" every morning (pushing me to work), every evening (pushing me to escape), every relationship (pushing me to cling or flee), and every threat (pushing me to fight or cower).

1. Divine Displeasure

"God loves me so much. I don't think he likes me, though."
"I don't measure up to God's standard of a 'good Christian.'"
"God would admit he hated me, if he could."

"Because of your hard and impenitent heart you are storing up wrath for yourself" (Romans 2:5). Yup. Not surprised. God can feel like a goliath, pulsing with frustration, tearing to shreds any scrap of dignity or self-respect we bring to the table. "You think you're a good person? Look at the cross. That's what you deserve: a bloody beating, and a shameful death in front of your family and friends. Nothing more. You're terrible, and you should think you're terrible." Okay. I do.

2. Self-Punishment

"I'm so stupid."
"I wish someone would just stab me,
          and drag me through the mud."
"I deserve this tragedy. It's my fault."

We do terrible things. We hurt other people. We hurt and embarrass ourselves. We misjudge. "The companion of fools will suffer harm" (Proverbs 13:20). It's not a stretch to wake up feeling like the fool day after day, harming those around us with our cemented habits, our secret desires, our sin spilling over into the lives and hearts of others. We want to take a samurai sword to our rotting souls and cut off our ugly pieces. When our self-disgust reaches a certain threshold, even we cannot resist taking the executioner's axe to our hearts, which we pronounce horrible and hideous.

3. Inadequacy

> "Everybody sees how pathetic I am."
> "I am undesirable."
> "If you made a movie about my life,
>   it would be an underperforming indie film
>   about being irredeemably pathetic."

We sense the lingering eyes of our neighbors. We feel the compulsion to make some gesture to scratch our itch of embarrassment: "I *know*. I know. I know. I'm overweight. I'm stupid. I'm less than _____. I'm imperfect." "You don't have to have a public hanging — I'll do it myself, somehow."

4. Comparison

> "I wish I had whiter teeth."
> "I wish I told better jokes."
> "I should be a better Christian."
> "There is a *reason* I'm not married and making six figures."

If I can't be the *best*, I don't want to *be*. I want to be the smartest, funniest, most attractive guy in the room. That is hardly ever the case. If I'm not the best, self-hatred jolts through my veins like electricity, and I kick into self-improvement mode. Too often I'm bested by a peer. He is a better boyfriend. A better employee. A better Christian. A better friend. A healthier sinner might hate the better person, but I quickly rush to the emotion underneath it all — self-disgust.

Comparative self-hatred, like a fossil fuel, has become the accepted energy of our rapid growth, blasting us toward perfection and destroying our basic structures of personal integrity at the same time. The virus of life-hacking flaunts a parade of benefits, until we find ourselves with a completely lost sense of our own humanity, purging our dinner and googling "six pack fast" at 12:30am.

5. Quitterism

"I hate my life."
"I might as well give up."
"I could try, or I could go home and binge watch my show."

"Low self-esteem and aiming low—they go together. Like the chicken and the egg."[2] There is a chasm between our desired self, and the real — the habits, desires, practices, status, and body in Men's Health Magazine, and our real habits, desires, practice, status, and body. We see the unchanging gap, year after year, between the "ideal me" and the *real me.*

So we quit. We call in to our self-hatred for the calculations: "Don't try. You'll embarrass yourself." Deal. I'll settle for calculated loss over failure's punch in the face any day. I'd rather make my own dunce cap and put it on when I get up in the morning than risk the chance I could genuinely earn it. And when our souls make us choose between perfection and insignificance, we are left feeling both imperfect and insignificant. We are left with nothing but our self-disgust to keep us warm, without the power to fix what disgusts us. And one day, eventually, this stubborn knife-wound gaping in our sensitive hearts sprouts a shoot of despair.

---

[2] Anneli Rufus, *Unworthy: How to Stop Hating Yourself* (New York: Penguin, 2014), 194.

God and Our Self-Hatred

It sometimes feels as if we must choose between self-hatred and high-handed narcissism. God rejects both options. We hate ourselves, because we have learned to do so from the world around us. It's easy to think that God hates us too — why wouldn't he? Yet, he is the one who wants to address our self-hatred with truth in love — to acknowledge our evil with the Spirit, forgive our evil with blood, and to dissolve our self-hatred in water: "For there are three that testify, the Spirit and the water and the blood; and the three are in agreement" (1 John 5:7). And he weaves his healing gospel through every stitching that marks our habitual self-mutilation. He has something to say to us, when we will insist on only speaking badly of ourselves. Here are five things God gives us when we hate ourselves:

1. Balanced Growth

> "Growth is balanced.
> Black and white thinking is the enemy."

We are often not *merely* self-haters. We love to *pity* ourselves as well. We are active minds caught in a violent back-and-forth between self-love and self-forgiveness. We rip ourselves to shreds, but lick our wounds protectively and worshipfully. Like alcohol and caffeine swirling around in our souls — a brutal back-and-forth of downers and uppers, critiquing each other and requiring each other — self-hate and self-love have become our only illusion of stability in a culture of oddly radical criticism and acceptance.

God hates it. God sees our exhausted and voracious lust for self-definition and utterly rejects all of it: "Your sons have fainted, They lie helpless at the head of every street, Like an antelope in a net, Full of the wrath of the LORD, The rebuke of your God." (Isaiah 51:20) God rebukes our mutilating self-rebukes, and he heals us from our worshipful self-healing.

Redemption works to slow the momentum of our ping-ponging between our own wrath and love, because it hijacks energy from the basic operating system that God gave us to grow and change. Our internal chaos will brand God both pushy and irrelevant at the same time — an ironic symptom of our own self-contradicting dialectic. We hate ourselves, so we scoff at God's love. We love ourselves, so we chafe at his discipline. Without it, our only cure for self-hatred will be high handed self-indulgence. Our internal engine is overheating at 10,000 RPM, but our souls are changing at a rate of 2mph because we confuse psychological intensity with spiritual growth.

We don't need God's love to correct our self-hatred, or his wrath to critique our self-love. We need his whole person — Jesus Christ, crucified for our evil and raised for our blessing and active hope — to rescue us from our desperate cycle completely for the sake of our growth as human beings. We need God to wound our self-wounding: "Faithful are the wounds of a friend; profuse are the kisses of an enemy" (Proverbs 27:6) — this is even more true when we profusely kiss ourselves, enslaved to kisses, intolerant of all wounds but those we self-inflict.

"Let a righteous man strike me—it is a kindness; let him rebuke me—it is oil for my head; let my head not refuse it." (Psalm 141:5) God works against the grain of our contorted cycle. But he has two responses: giving people over to their evil, and taking them out of it: "Those whom I love, I reprove and discipline, so be zealous and repent." (Revelations 3:19) His wrath should not cause your self-hatred. And his love should not cause self-excuse. "His law is love, and his gospel is peace." God gives us salvation, not from heavy-handed self-hate nor from shallow self-acceptance, but through giving us a better foundation for our self-criticism and self-acceptance. With God in view, we can trade our cycles of self-killing and self-coddling for a positive cycle of self-criticism and self-care. Christ offers consistent and rooted assessments of who we are in union with him — not wavering identities based upon our own imaginations and behaviors.

2. Self-Laughter

"Can I just laugh at how terrible I am?
Like, honestly laugh?"

In an interview with Stephen Colbert, Joel Osteen was promoting his book *The Power of I Am.*[3] Osteen explains the premise of his book — "I think a lot of people don't realize it, but playing in their mind [is] … 'I am slow.' 'I am unlucky.' 'I am not attractive.' And I think we're inviting negative things in. I think we're supposed to say, 'You know what? I'm blessed.' 'I'm strong.' 'I'm healthy.' 'I'm talented.' I think you have to invite the right things into your life." So here, Osteen is handcuffing his listeners with seriousness. And to a degree he is right — "Death and life are in the power of the tongue" (Prov. 18:21).

Osteen finishes by explaining, "I think people don't realize how many times we speak negative things about ourselves."

Colbert quips back, "I do that all the time, I'm so stupid." … and the entire crowd erupted in laughter. Why? For the same reason that an old man can look back on mistakes he made that caused him extreme amounts of self-hatred as a twentysomething, he now laughs about as the folly of his youth. Colbert kept going: "As a Catholic, let me ask you this: Have you ever tried the power of crippling guilt?" Laughter again.

The things which we internalize as existentially serious twentysomethings become trivial as we face death, responsibility, and consequences later in life. And if there is one principle I have found consistent, it is this: the more suffering someone has experienced, the better of a sense of humor they have about their past. "Remember also your Creator in the days of your youth, before the evil days come and the years draw near of which you will say, 'I have no pleasure in them'" (Ecclesiastes 12:1).

Comedy and tragedy is the great binary of a full life, and in God's drama which he is playing out in your life, you would be remiss to insist on its sadness at the expense of the ironic, the droll, the inane, the

---

[3] Joel Osteen, *The Power of I Am: Two Words That Will Change Your Life Today* (Nashville, NTL FaithWords, 2015). Interview on *The Tonight Show With Stephen Colbert* here: https://www.youtube.com/watch?v=GSsSD8ptLiA. I was half-way through this chapter when I saw this interview and realized: "My chapter is not much different from what Osteen is saying," and it led to serious revision. Osteen's work is not much different from the empty positive self-talk used by Bill Murray's character in *What About Bob?*, who repeats to himself while sick and miserable, "I feel good. I feel great. I feel wonderful." There is no real, material difference between Osteen's 2015 self-help and this 1991 comedic scene.

laughable of the illogical.[4] God's response to the absurdity of rebellion is not merely anger or grief, but laughter: "He who sits in the heavens laughs; the Lord holds them in derision" (Psalm 2:4).[5]

What does that look like, exactly? To sit back, after you sunk all your savings into moving to Dallas to marry the girl of your dreams, only to break up a month later, and drive 16 hours to Chicago with no money for gas to get home, collapse into your best friend's arms, cry … and then laugh. Not because it's funny, but because pain is absurd. Our grief can cause us to grant more rationality to absurdity than it deserves, leading us to indulge in self-hatred — that is, to pay for an explanation of negativity in the universe with our own value. Laughter is grief's equally legitimate response to suffering and shortcoming. "Even in laughter the heart may ache, and the end of joy may be grief" (Proverbs 14:13).

I sat at my Father's grave, after years of repressing and hating and suffering and self-blaming … and laughed — not *at* his death, but at the fact that it took me three years longer than my Dad had in him in order to reconcile with him. Laughter is not appropriate all the time — there is still a fine line between absurd and macabre. But our failures — our flunking out, our getting fired, our getting dumped, our expanding waist lines, our balding heads, our sagging circles under our eyes, our wrinkling faces — they deserve laughter and seriousness in the face of self-hatred. Self-laughter can be the perspective God grants those who merely need a balanced perspective on their own self-attitude: "Then our mouth was filled with laughter, and our tongue with shouts of joy; then they said among the nations, 'The Lord has done great things for them'" (Psalm 126:2).

3. Forgiveness

"Any shortcomings I *do* have: I'm forgiven.
God, help me to *really* believe that."

---

[4] It requires a concerted effort to reclaim the narrative structure of *commedia* as the story of our own lives — a way of understanding our own story *as farce*, that neither gives power to the bad nor the good, but empowers the ludicrous that often constitutes life-lived its deserved critique of seriousness which characterizes both self-hate and self-love.

[5] The "high comedy of Christ" is a play on "the hilarious unexpectedness of things rather than at their tragic expectedness." Frederick Buechner, *Telling the Truth: The Gospel as Tragedy, Comedy, and Fairy Tale* (San Francisco: Harper SanFrancisco, 1977), 61.

When we sin, we hate ourselves. Maybe not immediately, but eventually. It seeps in, through the cracks of our prideful self-fortification. Self-hatred is the inescapable symptom of every sin. We hurt a family member. We sin against our own bodies. We cause trouble for a friend. We embarrass those who love us. And we want to pay our emotional penance. We think, "If I could just filet enough of my soul to pay for that idiotic move, I will settle my karmic debt."

Thousands of Christians have performed the *scala sancta* — the "Holy Stairs" on which Jesus supposedly ascended to his trial before Pontius Pilate — a Roman Catholic relic, where Catholics climb the stairs on their knees to appease God's wrath. We resonate with that in our souls so deeply: "Yes. Give me something to climb. Give me pain that means forgiveness. Grant me some tangible action that gives me some control over my guilt. Then my self-hatred will have to wrestle my quantifiable penance."[6]

God has already wrestled your guilt. The weight we feel when we hate ourselves for real evil is the *very reality* that God sought to remove by his coming, and will forever remove by his coming again. "I, even I, am he who blots out your transgressions, for my own sake, and remembers your sins no more." (Isaiah 43:25) No more. Not guilt. Not your sins. "God continues to forgive the sins of those who are justified."[7] They're not a barrier. He doesn't hold them against you. That's hard to believe. And it's even more real than the paper and ink in front of you.

4. Self-Love

"I need to learn:
The Gospel *commands* us to love ourselves."

---

[6] On one account, Luther climbed the stairs and expressed doubt about its efficacy when he reached the top: "Who knows whether this prayer will avail?" Yet, according to his son Paul, while on the *scala sancta*, Luther heard a thunderous voice from heaven recalling the quotation of Habbakuk 2:4 in Romans 1:17: "The righteous shall live by faith," which caused him to flee the steps in shame. Rufus M. Jones, *Spiritual Reformers in the 16ᵗʰ & 17ᵗʰ Centuries* (New York: Macmillan, 1914), 5, n2.
[7] London Baptist Confession 11.5.

Self-love, in the modern sense, stands in stark contrast with the gospel.[8] If we are the sufficient source of our own love, then God's relevance to the self-hater is muted. Self-hate, when pitted against self-love, simply becomes a Kraken — a natural element that takes hold of us and thrashes us until we surrender to despair and death. Any self-hater who is told "love yourself" will soon know what it feels like to be crushed by hopelessness.

And yet, self-love *as a benefit of Jesus Christ* can become the axis of peace in a self-disgusted heart. Do you sense some profound lack in yourself — physically, spiritually, morally, comparatively? "You shall not take vengeance or bear a grudge against the sons of your own people, but you shall love your neighbor as yourself: I am the Lord." (Leviticus 19:18)

As yourself. Jesus nails the second greatest commandment to the wall with "as yourself" (Mark 12:30–31). Paul and James hang the entire "fulfillment of the law" on the wall with "as yourself" (Galatians 5:14; James 2:8).[9] Love your neighbor ... *as yourself*. It's easy to think of grace *received* as a God-to-us reality, and grace *that we give* as an us-to-others thing, each with an emphasis on *God* and *others*. And the self is simply a non-category, an empty pot with no dignity or rights or value.

---

[8] Here, most theologians are rightly scared that we will try to solve self-hatred with Narcissism. America's victimhood culture, which has used pride as a medicine for pain, evinces the slippery slope of narcissism, dwelling discreetly in the seed of secular self-compassion. And yet, the notion that self-love doesn't work with God should not compel us to reject the concept altogether — in fact, it should move us to reject the notion for the most part. More below.

[9] Calvin takes Galatians 5:14 to say, in essence, that you must love your neighbor *instead of* yourself, since the love of self and love of neighbor "are opposite and contradictory; for love (*amor*) of ourselves begets a neglect and contempt of others, it begets cruelty, it is the fount of avarice, of violence, deceit and all kindred vices, it drives us to impatience and arms us with the desire for revenge. The Lord therefore demands that it be changed to love (*charitatem*)." John Calvin, *The Epistles of Paul the Apostle to the Galatians, Ephesians, Philippians and Colossians*, Calvin's Commentaries, trans. T. H. L. Parker, ed. David W. Torrance and Thomas F. Torrance (Grand Rapids, MI: William B. Eerdmans Publishing Company, 1965), 101. He also comments on Leviticus 19:18, "φιλαυτία (self-love) blinds us so much as to be the parent of all iniquities." John Calvin, *Commentaries on the First Book of Moses*, trans. John King (Grand Rapids, MI: Eerdmans 1948), 369.

Some Christians might whack us on the head with a commonsense notion, which I believe is mistaken, that the right practice of the doctrine of total depravity is self-hatred. No. That's not good Calvinism.[10] The right practice of total depravity is not self-hatred, but *sober self-love*.[11] Total depravity highlights our inclination to receive and give grace selfishly.

Self-love seems rather to be the *challenge* which total depravity poses to the Christian — to practice a level of self-love which maintains those fundamental structures of humanity that obtain and dispense love with an orientation toward God's glory and the wellbeing of our neighbor. Without self-love, God-love and neighbor-love become vicious cycles of co-dependence — and this is not a capitulation to a secular self-help maxim, but an inwrought principle of the gospel.[12] "He who is forgiven little, loves little."[13]

So, Calvin takes Paul to say that if positive self-regard is *in any way* a standard for our love of others, we make sin our source and standard of obedience, which should be unallowable. I think Calvin, in these commentaries, excludes meaning from the text which is really there, simply for the sake of taking a shot at Roman Catholics at the Sorbonne, who advocated a Harvard sense of humanist self-love, not dissimilar from our modern individualistic selfishness. Evidence for my evaluation of Calvin appears when Jesus inescapably makes the point that Calvin is trying to reject in Galatians 5:14, in Matthew 7:12: "So whatever you wish that others would do to you, *do also* to them, for this is the Law and the Prophets." The assumption of a positive sense of self-love is inescapable here. On this passage, Calvin admits a distinction between the category of "self-love" (φιλαυτία) and "inordinate self-love," by which men "efface the rectitude which is engraven on their hearts." So, this term "inordinate" implies some sense of "ordinary," or non-grotesque self-love which Calvin allows. It is better, therefore, to allow Calvin's comments here on Matthew 7:12 to direct us to his better commentary on Galatians 5:14, when he says, "the image of God ought to be a specially sacred bond of union. Thus, no distinction is made between friend and foe, for the wickedness of men cannot annul the right of nature" (*Galatians*, 101).

[10] John Piper defends a "certain kind" of self-love, which he gets from Edwards, and he says is the very material of Christian hedonism. *Future Grace: The Purifying Power of the Promises of God* (Colorado Springs, CO: Multnomah, 1995, 2012), 391-392.

[11] The binary of "selfish" and "selfless" is guilty of the fallacy of the excluded middle — it insists on morally polarizing two concepts as the only two legitimate options of self-understanding. Yet, as we noted earlier, God does not want us to love ourselves or hate ourselves, but to *take his cue* in his attitude toward us, which is one that recognizes dignity, freely and liberally applies love, and practices uncompromising honesty about our sins and shortcomings.

[12]: "The friendliness one has toward another comes from the friendliness one has toward oneself." Thomas Aquins, III Sent., dist. 29, a. 3, ad 3.

[13] "Love your neighbor as yourself" is not a backwards play on our own sinful desires [i.e., "Stop loving yourself so much and start loving others," as if the two needed to be contrasted], but a play on the inescapable reality that as much as we need to be shrewdly self-critical, we must be cautiously self-compassionate.

More than that: "True humility also is not found by struggling to straddle the fence between egotistical vanity and self-hatred."[14] There is grace to be found in self-love. Scripture does not critique our self-care, but rather pushes us find grace in it. "To be self-affirming yet self-forgetful, positive yet realistic, grace-filled and unpretentious—that is the Christian vision of abundant life."[15]

God doesn't hate your waist size. He isn't making fun of your salary with the angels in heaven. He doesn't make fun of your bad jokes. He doesn't hate your social awkwardness. Like any good father, he just wants you to be happy — "I have no greater joy than to hear that my children are better, more secure, more stable, more admired, more impressive children than all the other children." Actually, no. "I have no greater joy than to hear that my children are walking in the truth." (3 John 1:4). God wants to ground the tension between our satisfaction and our ambition — your self-compassion and self-criticism — in his daily call and care for you.

God finds joy when we look to Him, in the times when we are running fast towards Him and in the times of repentance (when we slowly turn to Him with humble, grace-hungry eyes). He longs for our joy to be found in Him and for His name to be glorified in our finding joy in him (something that can occur in the midst of our "successes" *and* our "failures").

5. Tenacity

"It's time to start bullying my self-hatred."

"For I am confident of this very thing, that He who began a good work in you will perfect it until the day of Jesus Christ" (Philippians 1:6). Do you want to discover a new way of living? Are you sick and tired of being sick and tired? Scratch this on a Post-It note, and stick it on your computer:

---

[14] David G. Myers and Malcom A. Jeeves, *Psychology Through the Eyes of Faith* (New York: HarperCollins, 2003), 173.
[15] Ibid., 174.

1. Give up.

2. Don't give up.

Jot it on your hand. Carve it into your desk. Say it out loud. Now, look at your fears. Your failures. Your sources of self-hatred. Your dark voices. Your spiritual sickness. Your utter inability to believe a good grand story about yourself. Then re-read Philippians 1:6. What adjectives do we have? "Confident." "Good." "Perfect." Those are things God is doing in you.

Strike out *Give up.*[16] Find the good in your life. Listen to the one person who is your unceasing champion — a dad, a mom, a grandpa or grandma, someone who is a better friend to you than you are. God gives us those people because he hates self-hatred. I guarantee that she tells you things that God will tell you on the last day:

"I'm crazy."
  "I created you to feel deeply."
"I'm pathetic."
  "I was in control over your failure."
"I'm unlovable."
  "I love you so much, and I created people to love you."
"I'm destined to be just like my mom/dad."
  "I gave you today, because I don't believe that."
"I'm weak."
  *"That is a hard, unrecognizably beautiful reality
  that I created for the sake of our fellowship."*
"I'm worthless."
  *"I created you with the same intimacy
  that I created Adam and Eve."*
"I can't stop."
  "I don't love you less; I will help you to get back up."
"I'm hopeless."

---

[16] This technique is found in the amazing book *Unworthy: How to Stop Hating Yourself,* by Anneli Rufus. The book is worth buying and reading in its entirety. Self-haters may read it in a single sitting.

"You can't see your future in this darkness,
but I can. It's not easy. But it's meaningful."
"I deserve to be hurt."
"Vengeance is mine, and I don't want you to hurt yourself.
I want to hug you."
"I should kill myself."
"I breathed life into you for a purpose. And this is not it."
"I can't do this forever."
"I will complete the good work I started in you."

Conclusion

God fights alongside us. He doesn't fight for our superficial self-compassion, or our destructive self-disgust. He comes alongside us and, sword in hand, commands us to abandon our self-protection and our self-indulgence. The place where he encounters us — our very persons — is holy ground. He battles our self-hatred by calling us to worship — at so many times and places and ways, with his incalculable resources.

We feel like those resources don't exist. We despair under the weight of our constant, constant, constant self-hatred. Our internal voices smack us around when we submit to them. And they laugh at us when we fight back. "In return for my love they accuse me, but I give myself to prayer." (Psalm 109:4) God, our suitor, the one who loves us, fights with us. Tell that to your self-hatred next time you wake up and hear the whisper, "Another day of being the ugliest, the unobserved, the middle of the pack, the insignificant, the forgotten, the unloved, the scorned…"

Yeah, maybe. But those realities are fleeting — they come, they go, they rise and fall, and eventually come to pass for all. But God is really with you today, alongside you, fighting with you. Tell the voice, with full divine authority, to shut its mouth. Christ claims you today, and will not let go.

If you want something to sink your teeth into, one specific prayer might be worth a try: "The Prayer of Humble Access."

This prayer may feel removed, irrelevant, unrelated, flat, false, unhelpful, and even pretentious. It shouldn't be easy to pray. It's not an easy prayer. But it is not pietism nor legalism. It does not require an unrelenting dialectic between self-hatred and self-forgiveness. It names what we already know, but will not admit. It names our *own* pretension—it relinquishes our own sense of self-importance and entitlement, the root of personal retrogression.[17] To say "I am not worthy" does not entail what religious communities require: "I am scum." No. It names our need for something more than ourselves to help us "to become conformed to the image of His Son" (Rom 8:29).

It names something concrete and specific—that God has assumed the same realities which we feel cursing our bones every day: flesh, blood, mystery—but his body drags us out of the deep. He is the only one who will acknowledge our souls need washing, and at the same time promise never to leave us because of our sin. Whatever our first impression of God—whether an empty concept, a failed strategy, a pretentious judge who wants us to be involved in his clique—he is *anything* but abstract. And you are part of a long history of self-hating Christians that God will one day redeem from the twisted darkness of self-hatred. Pray this out loud. Don't let your quiet mind rob your vocal body of the chance to approach the Lord's table. Let us pray:[18]

---

[17] Timothy Radcliffe comments: "Jesus's delight in us is not vacuous affirmation: it is our painful joy in being stripped of our pretension." Timothy Radcliffe, *What is the Point of Being a Christian?* (New York: Burns & Oats, 2006), 62.

[18] Some of this language is updated from the modernized 1548 version. Found in Gordon Jeanes, "Cramner and Common Prayer," in *The Oxford Guide to the Book of Common Prayer: A Worldwide Survey*, ed. Charles Hefling and Cynthia Shattuck (New York: Oxford University Press, 2006), 25 [21-38].

The Prayer of Humble Access

We do not presume to come to
this thy Table, O merciful Lord
trusting in our own righteousness,
but in thy manifold and great mercies.
We be not worthy so much as
to gather up the crumbs under thy Table.
But thou art the same Lord,
whose desire is always to have mercy:
Grant us therefore, gracious Lord,
so to eat the Flesh of thy dear Son Jesus Christ,
and to drink his Blood, in these holy Mysteries,
that we may continually dwell in him,
and he in us, that our sinful bodies
    may be made clean by his Body,
and our souls washed through his most precious Blood.
Amen.

Chapter 8
Doubt

I should be tempted to forget,
I fear, the Crown of Rule,
The Scales of Trade, the Cross of Faith,
As Hardly worth renewal.

For these have governed in our lives,
And see how men have warred.
The Cross, the Crown, the Scales may all
As well have been the Sword.[1]
      —Robert Frost

Faith never disappears. Despite its public image, it is actually quite fragile, easily turning sour. The backslidden and apostate are not empty people. They're quite full. Usually, with bitterness; and some relief — they experience faith more like a splinter than a succor. Three years ago, I witnessed my own faith spoil in the timespan of a single hymn.

Within a period of six months:

- My dad unexpectedly died.
- My sexual sin came to light in my community.
- People started spreading false rumors about that sin.
- I lost job prospects and writing opportunities because of those rumors.
- I moved to Dallas for a girl.
- Said girl and I broke up.

---

[1] Robert Frost, "The Peaceful Shepherd," in Edward Connery Lathem (ed.) *The Poetry of Robert Frost* (New York: Henry Holt and Company, 1969), 252.

I drove back from Dallas to Chicago the day we broke up. And to Philadelphia days later — Easter Sunday. I remember sitting in Easter Sunday service, in Philadelphia, singing some hymn about Christian victory, realizing — through the first, second, third chorus of *Christ the Lord is Risen Today*, or some other God-awful major key cacophany — that my faith was wheezing its last breath. I've seen too much not to believe in God. But I was done. I don't know the exact moment I became a Christian. But I know the *exact* moment I stopped believing he is good.

One man explains that, after his brother committed suicide, "For a year I said nothing to God and he said nothing to me."[2] That explains it well. I imagined myself locking eyes with God and throwing up my hands: "That's it. I'm out." All the sadness became funny, just for a moment. And I had the sense that God, like a passive-aggressive boyfriend, wanted out just as much as I did.[3]

Five Aspects of Doubt

Each of our experiences with doubt looks different. It is necessary to begin with a definition, as we move forward.

> ## Definition:
>
> *Doubt bred in suffering is the suspicion that Jesus Christ is malicious or indifferent to me.*

[2] David G. McNeish, "Grief is a Circular Staircase: The Uses and Limits of Models of Grief in the Pastoral Care of the Bereaved," *Practical Theology*, 6, no. 2 (2013): 198 [190-203].
[3] I should say that it has been, is, and always will be *chic* to doubt Christianity. In our societies and in our hearts, there will always be a group that celebrates suspicion toward God as a virtue. It is really, as Dave Eggers points out, a function of immaturity: "Young men love martyrdom. You get to be the victim and the hero at the same time." Dave Eggers, *Your Fathers, Where Are They? And the Prophets, Do They Live Forever?* (New York: Vintage Books, 2015), 111. The victim and the hero — doubt gives us the opportunity to be God's "victims," and it is with this basic theological sense which we will deal in this chapter. It is simply worth noting that this inclination *is* "cool," and always will be, which I think should give us pause about the credibility of the instinct's content. But that is really an aside.

Doubt, of course, is more than uncertainty. We have many Bible passages that assure the uncertain, making space for Christian doubt. Our twenties are a more potent form of doubt than we faced in our second decade. Teenage doubt is usually "evidentialist doubt," anxiety over the existence of God. Most of us who doubt in our twenties *affirmed* the existence of God in our adolescence. Now, we face not evidential doubt, but existential doubt — now that we are certain of God's existence, what do we make of all the trouble he causes?

Armed even with the most eloquent argumentation in the world, suspicion about God always patrols our hearts, like an alien sentinel exploring some unwelcome creature into its midst. Doubt finds the theological certainties which make suffering less bearable repugnant and untidy; inconsiderate and unwelcome; betraying and unknowing. The problem of doubt in the life of the twentysomething, then, is not a problem of science but of suffering.

There are several sources of our evolved twentysomething doubt.

1. Trauma

The traumatized are often the religiously disaffected.
We are not dealing with "evidences" for God.
This is personal.
The doubts are as splintered and complex as the people.

The traumatized, like a child with a bruised rib, look at God and wonder why. There is often a short season of devotion, followed by disavowal. The demands of a perfect God impress impractical ultimatums on the abused. Distrust of the powerful is a common virus planted in the hearts and minds of the traumatized. And God is certainly powerful.

2. Absence

"Say something. I dare you."
"Please. I need you to speak."
"Say *anything*. I can't keep this going on my own.
      I need you to say something; do anything."

God has always left a letter for us to read in his absence. But we are often left wanting his presence — his embrace. "Looking around, doesn't look like you're any more present than anyone else who's not here." Life hits us with wave after wave after wave. Spurgeon "learned to kiss the wave that throws me against the Rock of Ages." Well, most doubters yearn to face the rock — but life feels more like an endless ocean of waves. No rock. No kiss. No nothing. "God might exist. Doesn't matter either way, it seems."

3. Calvinism

> "You've done enough, thank you."
> "And you didn't stop this, because…?"
> "Sure, you run my life.
>   But are you there to help me, or make me feel guilty?"

Calvinism — with a heavy emphasis on God's work, in creation and salvation — can take on a dark side in the midst of suffering. "My yoke is easy, and my burden is light" (Matt 11:30). But we know what people mean when they speak of the "weight" of God's sovereignty — the heft of his hand; the entailments of his control; the implications of his nuanced involvement in our tragedy; the offense of his meticulous care for creation against our suffering.

It's hard to feel like Jesus's yoke is easy when we witness our faith taking its last breath, and he's holding a smoking gun. It's not easy to pretend that the solid line between our every event and God's direct, decisive planning is easy. Sometimes that solid line becomes bold enough to bulldoze lament into hatred. And there have been times when I have hated God for his sovereignty.

4. Exhaustion

> "God simply isn't relevant anymore."
> "I tried. I really tried. And I just ran out of faith."
> "This isn't helping.
>   I need to focus my efforts on things that help."

We hear them calling now — our Christian friends and relatives, asking us to prove our case: "Well what do you hope to gain by giving up on God?" We never have an answer. "Something *else*."[4] The doubters are a weary people. "I don't believe" is often a station at which we do not arrive for a decade. "I don't care" is the way. It's the safest place for the tired who have experienced even the best of Christianity as only a ladder to climb.

5. Hypocrisy

"I don't care if God exists.
　　　If you believe in him, I don't want any part of it."
"These people just make it too complicated.
　　　I don't need more complicated."
"I don't feel comfortable with them.
　　　It isn't worth the risk."

It's easy to look at Christians and say the worst: "You are a nice person *in spite of* your Christianity." And if they're vicious, it's obviously because of it. We have made up our minds, but it's quite clear to us why — Christians *are* hypocrites. They are self-interested and ideological and double-minded and are on an agenda to convert. And we doubters won't forget it.

God and Our Misgivings About God

Can God redeem the wounded human who quivers in suspicious fear before his power? More than that: God accomplished redemption for precisely this sort of suspicion — the wounded, bitter, justified kind. John Calvin was at times terrified of God. Voices in his head would taunt him, "suggesting that God is our enemy because he is unfavorable

---

[4] "There is a time for departure even when there's no certain place to go!" Tennessee Williams, *Camino Real* (New York: New Directions, 1953), 71.

towards us." [5] Yes, Calvin. I feel that way. I don't consider myself a "doubter." I'd rather not be defined relative to the God who insists on both maximizing my pain and critiquing my grief — who both insists that I must simultaneously acknowledge he has decreed all of my misery, and that he is not responsible for any of it. Yes, "God is our enemy" — well put, Calvin. That thought *does* cross my mind when I do a little theological algebra.

This chapter is the most fresh for me, personally. So, I hope we can sit together through five ways that God encounters us doubters. We're not like doubting Thomas, who can find resolution by putting his finger in God's wounds. Quite the opposite: We doubt because we have caught God's finger *in our wounds*, tinkering around, slicing and dicing for our joy and his glory, apparently. Yes: "God, please speak now. What are you doing?"

In other chapters, we sat in a lot of Scripture. In this chapter, I want to sit with our friend John Calvin — fellow saint and student of Scripture. Scripture has a lot to say about doubt. And Calvin is a living example of much of that teaching, about 1500 years closer to us. Calvin is not inspired or authoritative, except that he gives us glimpses of a Spirit-led faith-in-the-midst-of-pain that seems neither shallow nor manic.

Calvin had an unwavering conviction in the sovereignty of God, in his hand in his own suffering, and yet faced death and grief and loss every day for decades. You don't need to become a Calvin scholar to sit with us. But I would like to introduce you to my faithful friend, whose reputation is grand, but whose grief is as hard and brittle as any of us. Sit with me in the same room as Calvin. I think that he was very much like us. God gives the doubtful five gifts.

1. A Realistic Faith

"Can we please be honest about
how brittle faith feels?"

"Faith" is a rather *forward* gift of God to the doubter. "I'm not sure I *want* to believe." While doubt is strong, Calvin does not allow its

---

[5] John Calvin, *Institutes of The Christian Religion*, 2 vols., tans. Ford Lewis Battles, ed. John T. McNeill (Louisville, KY: Westminster John Knox, 1960, 2006), 1:566 (3.2.21).

momentum to bulldoze his world entirely. Calvin insists, not only on the normalcy of doubt, but on the resiliency of faith. The most cunning trick of evil in our minds is not what folk mythology would tell us: "The greatest trick the devil pulled was convincing the world he doesn't exist." No.

The greatest trick evil has pulled is to convince the faithful that they don't have faith. "Faith, on the other hand, replies that while he afflicts us he is also merciful because his chastisement arises out of love rather than wrath."[6] We lash back at that claim. It *is* in our DNA to lash back at such claims. But that's where Calvin begins his understanding of doubt — not by critiquing it, but by normalizing it:

> "While we teach that faith ought to be certain and assured, we cannot imagine any certainty that is not tinged with doubt, or any assurance that is not assailed by anxiety. On the other hand, we say that believers are in perpetual conflict with their own unbelief."[7]

Yes. But wait. My doubts are *real*. I'm not sitting here praying, "I do believe; help my unbelief" (Mark 9:24). My prayers sound more like, "Stay out of my life" and "You're no longer welcome here" or "Show yourself!!" Understand me: I'm not asking the question, "What do we do with our doubts, as Christians?" I'm asking the question, "What do we do with our doubts, as sinners and sufferers?"

Calvin's point is that these voices and questions can exist in the same space as the heart in which God is working — the heart which God has united to Christ by faith: "For by grace you have been saved through faith. And this is not your own doing; it is the gift of God" (Eph. 2:8). The world around us throws Christians into "perpetual conflict." We are not troubled by the plausibility of God's nonexistence, but on the plausibility of his malicious existence — that his existence casts a shadow of punishment and negative value over *all* our sins and sufferings.

That, right there, is the boxing ring of faith. Choose: is your situation a product of God's love, or his wrath? If you choose wrath, you choose to disbelieve. If you choose love, you choose the far more difficult

---

[6] Ibid.
[7] Ibid., 1:562 (3.2.17).

path — it is a path of cognitive dissonance and very few answers and no "closed circles" of explanation. To choose wrath is to choose an explanation for our misery: God hates us. But to choose love is to sacrifice explanation for the sake of belief. Nobody ever told us we would have to make that trade when we became Christians. It's God-awful.

Yet, now we face the opportunity to believe: to hold in an open hand our need to trace a bold arrow of causality from God to our pain, along with a furrowed brow and hateful eyes on his face, all menacing like. Faith is the choice to lay down our theological sharpie. Never is that more painful than for the Calvinist. Yet, for those who find a way, it opens a new world of emotional possibility.

Calvin resorts to one phrase when the voices assail him: "Love, not wrath." "Love, not wrath." "Love, not wrath." God's free offer of grace by faith shines the spotlight on the reality that our decision to experience our suffering as God's wrath or grace one way or another is very much *our decision* — excruciating as that may be.

2. A Biblical Community

> "I can't continue believing with the wrong people
> and I can't do this without the right people."

God gifts doubters their own space to doubt. We've been hurt. Just because our questions are threatening God with the jagged edge of apostasy, that doesn't mean they're bad questions. Christian therapists often speak of the "counseling epidemic" among Christian twentysomethings, which may very well exist because of our victory-centered churches services.[8] We are looking for a place to find biblical expression of our innermost pains *in order* that we might hope, and not having found it in an Easter-centered evangelical culture, it's not hard to see the logic of many who seek hope elsewhere.

We find expression for despair in Scripture: "Why do you forget us forever, why do you forsake us for so many days?" (Lam 5:20) We find it in the counseling office. But rarely will we find that in church — even in a Good Friday service, which liturgically anticipates with well-intended earnestness the immanence of the resurrection, yet

---

[8] I am entirely indebted to Jenna Perrine for this phraseology and insight.

marginalizes those who cannot celebrate with a hearty "Hallelujah!"[9] Joy after grief is a beautiful moment for the resilient, but not all of us are so quick in our resiliency.

I don't often feel as though I belong in church. And my sense of unbelonging reflects my inwrought sense that I don't belong with God. The political power of "normal" has squeezed the margins of church-belonging into the space where doubters are formally welcomed, but materially rendered sub-belongers; only those willing to *celebrate* are genuinely included in the service that is considered a celebration.

Yet, God forges a different path, as Henri Nouwen explains: "A Christian community is therefore a healing community not because wounds are cured and pains are alleviated, but because wounds and pains become openings or occasions for a new vision."[10] Intimacy takes sharing joys and sorrows with each other, and if God commands human beings to be in community, then he must mean by this that he commands human beings to pursue intimacy: "Community emerges as the fruit of intimacy."[11] Nouwen, once again: "When loneliness is among the chief wounds of the minister ... Community arises where the sharing of pain takes place, not as a stifling form of self-complaint, but as a recognition of God's saving promises."[12]

The doubtful, of course, are suspicious of "God's saving promises." That's the whole point. And yet (and I can only speak for myself), I never have felt more at home in a church when I find that the pastor knows my pain. I suspect that the doubtful would feel at home in a church with a lonely pastor. I imagine that the church that laments is big enough for the doubter to breathe. If I walked into a church that had as much space for disbelief and double-mindedness among the saints as Scripture — "Gideon, Barak, Samson, Jepthah" (Heb. 11:32) — my suspicions about God would likely hold less power over my affections, knowing that God righteously shepherds even those sheep who suspect

---

[9] "It is likely that our theological problem in the church is that our gospel is a story believed, shaped, and transmitted by the dispossessed; and we are now a church of possessions for whom the rhetoric of the dispossessed is offensive and their promise is irrelevant. And we are left to see if it is possible for us again to embrace solidarity with the dispossessed." Walter Brueggemann, *Land: Place as Gift, Promise, and Challenge in Biblical Faith*, 2nd ed, Overtures in Biblical Theology (Minneapolis, MN: Fortress, 2002), 206.

[10] Henri Nouwen, *The Wounded Healer*, 94.

[11] Andrew Purves, *The Search for Compassion: Spirituality and Ministry* (Louisville, KY: Westminster John Knox, 1989), 124.

[12] Nouwen, *The Wounded Healer*, 94.

he is a butcher.

A biblical community gives us the opportunity to "borrow faith" for a season. There are many of us who will need to be carried into glory. And God is not ignorant of that. Moreover, that's *why* he created the church, and called it to "have
mercy on those who doubt" (Jude 1:22).

We are left asking with Calvin, "I am utterly exhausted by these melancholy thoughts all night long. . . . What else, therefore, dear brother, can we do than lament our calamity?"[13]

3. A Spacious Theology

"My spiritual adrenals are tapped."

One of the reasons we push God away is because of our trained tendency to over-spiritualize everything — that is, to require a spiritual response for everything, a theological reason for everything, a joyous and celebratory knee-jerk in every situation. We can perform those things for a while. But eventually, it may break. And when that over-spiritualizing shatters on the rocks of trauma, we write God off, as though he had endorsed our hyper-Christianity the whole time. Calvin didn't over-spiritualize his pain.

Calvin writes to his friend Viret, after Viret's wife has died, and he urges:

> "Come, on this condition, that you disengage your mind not only from grief, but also from every annoyance. Do not fear that I will impose any burden upon you, through my means you will be allowed to take whatever rest is agreeable to you. If any one prove troublesome to you, I will interpose. The brethren, also, make the same promise to you as I do. I will also be surety that the citizens do not interfere with your wishes."[14]

---

[13] John Calvin, "To Farel," Strasbourg, 24th October 1538," *Letters of John Calvin: Compiled from the Original Manuscripts and Edited with Historical Notes*, 4 vols., trans. David Constable, ed. Jules Bonnet (Edinburgh: Thomas Constable and Co., 1885), 1:76 [75-80].
[14] John Calvin, "To Viret, 8th March, 1546," *Letters of John Calvin*, 2:23-24.

Calvin's solution to grief is not "Pray more." Can the bereaved pray? Yes. But it's easy to have the sense that until we come to a "spiritual" resolution to our pain then, on a Christian account, it is not truly resolved. Yet, Calvin makes no mention of God in this letter. He mentioned in an earlier letter that he was praying for Viret's wife before she died, but on this occasion, this father of Calvinism — Calvin himself — simply says, "Come, on the condition that you take a vacation." Pastoral work at its finest?

Three years later, Calvin writes to Viret to inform him of the death of his own wife. He recounts the last moments he spent with her, and was with her when she died. Yet, again, Calvin doesn't mention God, except that his wife's dying words were her confession of trust in God to care for those closest to them.

> "Although the death of my wife has been exceedingly painful to me, yet I subdue my grief as well as I can. Friends, also, are earnest in their duty to me. It might be wished, in deed, that they could profit me and themselves more; yet one can scarcely say how much I am supported by their attentions. But you know well enough how tender, or rather soft, my mind is."[15]

The constant guilt over not being spiritual enough is enough to exhaust one of all charity toward God. Often, we run from God and Christianity because we feel like the screws are too tight — there is no space to breathe, to live, to grieve, to love, to risk, to cry, to lament, to complain. It's just hacking away at all our initial impulses: the mortification of the flesh. Much doubt arises within exhausted mortifiers.

But mortification is not the only tool of Christianity, or of Calvinism. We often get stuck in "salvation" gear, and forget that God expresses love for us in the present time and place with earthly graces. The pressure is not *always* on us to be higher and better and deeper and holier. It would serve our faith, and our doubts, "to move away from 'endism' to a more spirit-centered spirituality that values the present as both time and place, and that privileges life itself."[16]

---

[15] John Calvin, "To Viret, April 7, 1549," *Letters of John Calvin*, 2:202.
[16] Flora A. Keshgian, *Time for Hope: Practices for Living in Today's World* (New York: Continuum, 2006), 119.

Calvin practices this "commonplace" theology, not by ignoring God, but by knowing theologically that he doesn't have to over-spiritualize every experience. Perhaps in this way, our doubts can be soothed, not by resolving the trauma of life, or the contentious emotions that trauma elicits in us toward God, but by knowing that God isn't watching us suffer with a clipboard, critiquing the holiness of our painful screams. In Christian grief, we are freed from well-to-do Christian spiritualization of our suffering, because when it comes to suffering well, God gives no points for style.

4. A Better Philosophy

"Does God have to be either:
a meaningless oaf or a meaningful monster?"

God isn't mad at you for your doubts; he *wants* us to have a faith like a child. That doesn't mean that God desires naiveté. That means that we are often inquiring and scared and very, very, very suspicious and in need of assurance. How often does a child with loving parents question her or his security in this world, and the love of the parents? Quite often.

Calvin was pastoring people who had no understanding of Scripture. The result in their lives was not that they were *liberated* and free in their grief, because the heavy hand of Calvin's God was not on them. No. Rather, in the absence of the sovereign God, "every place was filled with superstitions."[17]

We live in a time similar to Calvin's, where everyone is a self-donned philosopher, promoting their own quotes and writings and online classes. We cling and package and popularize commonsense phraseology, text each other motivational quotes, and wonder why doubt arises in our hearts about the reliability of God at the first sign of trouble. For some of us, doubt is not a result of suffering exhausting our faith, but is the logical outcome of suffering working its havoc in our superstitious, life-hacking version of Christianity. While Calvin is silent about God in his letter to Viret, he has different words for Monsieur de Richebourg, about the death of his colleague:

---

[17] Hugh Young Reyburn, *John Calvin: His Life, Letters, and Work* (London: Hodder & Stoughton, 1914), 94.

"There is no ground, therefore, for those silly and wicked complaints of foolish men; O blind death! O hard fate! O implacable daughters of destiny! O cruel fortune! The Lord who had lodged him here for a season, at this stage of his career has called him away. What the Lord has done, we must, at the same time, consider has not been done rashly, nor by chance, neither from having been impelled from without, but by that determinate counsel, whereby he not only foresees, decrees, and executes nothing but what is just and upright in itself, but also nothing but what is good and wholesome for us. Where justice and good judgment reign paramount, there it is impious to remonstrate."[18]

Quite honestly, I find Calvin here to be very insensitive. This is a younger Calvin. A man in the "cage stage" of his own Calvinism — excited about an ideology that explains everything, deaf to the unexplainable things in the world. A pastor policing grief — how pathetically cliché. Too often, we get the sense that Calvinism is the desensitized and fatalistic determinism that ceaselessly reminds us of God's hand in tragedy — and too often, our instincts are right. We can scream our indictments at God about our grief, and call him responsible for our tragedies. And God takes it — as he did with Job, and the author of Lamentations and Ecclesiastes. *God wants that from us*. He doesn't want our "pious" confession — he wants our brutal honesty. He did not come and die on a cross so that we could *pretend* with him — so that we could play "Good little Evangelical" *with him who both ordains and is acquainted with grief*. He becomes the friend of doubters — not "merciful" as though he had to stay his frustration with us, but curious about our finitude; happy about our limits.

When my mom dies — and that will be a day when I go toe-to-toe with God — I can *at least* say, "This was not 'cruel chance.' You took her from me." And God will answer, "Yes, I did." My mom's own father died on the night of the lunar landing. And all the suffering and loneliness that she experienced because of that, he caused it — *he decreed it from his throne*.

---

[18] John Calvin, "To Monsieur de Richebourg, April 1541," *Letters of John Calvin*, 1:224 [222-229].

When she dies, I will hate him for it.

That sentence deserves to be unqualified. God *wants* us to be unqualified with him — bare and strong and brutal with him. Jacob was in his wrestling. Wrestling is not merciful. It is violent and disrespectful and conquering. Grief wrecks the integrity of all our niceties. And, in the best instances, it is our opportunity to pour out all our disrespect and distrust toward God. *It is there, after all, isn't it?*

This is the sticking point for your identity as a doubter, which we can take from Calvin. We are pit between the pagan philosophy of "foolish men" — "O blind death! O hard fate! O cruel fortune!" — and the "impious remonstrance" of bitterness toward God about the tragedy which he has struck upon us. And, for Calvin, it is better for us by God's mercy to be an impious remonstrant who is offended by God's agency in our pain than to be a fool who sees all our worst tragedies as meaningless accidents.

5. A Guaranteed End

"God will bring the end we all
expect him to bring today."

Our lives are intermingled with certainties and doubts, and even those mixtures change with seasons. Augustine. Luther. Kierkegaard. You and I. We are none of us unscarred by the world, at times glancing at God in spite and distrust — is it incompetence? Is it ill-will? Is he the cosmic trickster pulling the rug out from under us again, and again, and again, and again, and again, telling us to trust him *one more time?* Suffering is so prolonged in certain seasons that it feels as if life *forces our hand* in disbelief: "It is as if, in the aftermath of tragedy, hope cannot sustain itself."[19]

And yet, no Calvinist approach to twentysomething existential doubt would be complete without noting this basic reality: God hates evil, too. "*But you're saying he caused all of it.*" Yes, I am. And it's nearly impossible to imagine a reason that would justify his orchestration of the world as he has. But there will come a time when you will put your

---

[19] Kathleen H. O'Conner, *Lamentations and the Tears of the World* (Maryknoll, NY: Orbis, 2003), 29.

doubt aside. There will come a day when all the agencies of evil which we suffer, which we hate, for which we despise God's allowance, will be aggressively and ravenously pummeled into the ground. One day, God will brutally, ferociously aggressively, savagely, ravenously beat evil against the rocks
with his fists.

Calvin grieves the death of a friend:

"They have not gained the worth of a single hair by his death. For there stands before the judgment-seat of God a witness and avenger of their villainy, whose voice will proclaim their destruction more loudly than if it shook the earth. We, the survivors whom the Lord has left behind for a little while, let us persevere in the same path wherein our deceased brother walked until we have finished our course."[20]

Doubt is a wall we hit in mile 20 of the marathon. We are exhausted. Our weaknesses and superficialities are coming up empty. We are gasping for air, witnessing our faith suffer on the ground. "Let us persevere in the same path." Because as much as we hate this journey, and as much as we feel unsatisfied by the spoiler we receive in the book of Revelation, *we will rest, and we will be satisfied.* And that is the end which God promises to us, sufferers of evil, only on earth because we are "survivors whom the Lord has left behind for a little while." In my better moments (or my more naïve moments), I like that.

Conclusion

It is human to suffer, just as it is our common situation as fallen humans to suspect God of foul play. Doubt is a very normal, Christian thing:

---

[20] John Calvin, "To Farel," Strasbourg, 24th October 1538," *Letters of John Calvin*, 1:76 [75-80]. I had never cried reading Calvin before, until I read this just now, reading his consolation of Farel over the death of Courault.

"The godly heart feels in itself a division because it is partly imbued with sweetness from its regeneration of divine goodness, partly grieves in bitterness from an awareness of its calamity; partly rests upon the promise of the gospel, partly trembles at the evidence of its own iniquity; partly rejoices at the expectation of life, partly shudders at death. This variation arises from imperfection of faith, since in the course of the present life it never goes so well with us that we are wholly cured of the disease of unbelief and entirely filled and possessed by faith. Hence arise these conflicts, when unbelief, which reposes in the remains of the flesh, rises up to attack the faith that has been inwardly conceived."[21]

What Calvin says *does* explain all of us, no matter how strong or weak we think our faith actually is. Normalizing doubt doesn't quite accomplish a satisfying treatment of those doubts, yet treating them with answers can feel like a compromise of their normalcy.

I live among the bones and ashes of past relationships, past memories, past opportunities, and a passed parent — death has taken its toll, and there is no "resurrection" happening anywhere that I can see.

Yet, the basic truth is this: in this life, resurrection can take minutes, and it can take years. Healing is not something that can be expected of us. God heals us with faith, community, a minimalist spirituality, meaningfulness, and a promise to end our suffering — some of these long things, some of them short. One way or another, we must address our doubts, not as obviously justified or obviously sinful, but as an obvious sign that we are in need of some kind of healing. "We have to live the theological reality of new life in Christ in such a way that we are always being healed. Either we are being healed of our own suffering or compassion will become increasingly impossible for us."[22]

---

[21] John Calvin, *Institutes*, 1:564 (3.2.18).
[22] Andrew Purves, *The Search for Compassion*, 84.

Chapter 9
Grief

Let my snow-tracks lead
on, on. Let them, where they stop,
stop. There, in mid-field.[1]

"At the upper entrance they hacked
   the wooden trellis with axes." (Psalm 74:5)

   "Safe" is hard to feel; to remember.

"And then, with hatchets and hammers,
   they smashed all its carved work." (Psalm 74:6)

   Relationships with our parents become
   embittered, strained, distant.

"They set your sanctuary on fire;
   they desecrated the dwelling place of your name,
   bringing it to the ground." (Psalm 74:7)

   Innocence is lost beyond doubt,
   beyond reach, in the clasp of regret.

"They said to themselves, 'We will utterly subdue them';
   they burned all the meeting places of God in the land.
We do not see our emblems. . . ." (Psalm 74:8–9).

   "Home" no longer symbolizes "safe,"
   but "trapped" and "doomed."

---

[1] Hayden Carruth, "*from* The Clay Hill Anthology," in *The Art of Losing: Poems of Grief and Healing* (New York: Bloomsbury, 2010), 268 [267-268].

For some of us, *any* loss — any death — is a signal flare: everything is lost.[2] Like a television show that decides to kill a main character, our twenties write disturbing wreckage into our plotlines. But these characters are real life. They provide continuity and meaning to our yesterdays, and our tomorrows. And now their absence haunts us.

Five Aspects of Our Grief

> **Definition:**
>
> *Grief is the pain felt by the wound of loss.*

And loss *is* a wound. Like the deep scrape of a motorcycle accident — to the bone — or losing a limb.[3] Loss isn't physical death. It can be. But there are at least five losses that we experience in our twenties. These losses cast our lives as a slowly deteriorating, dilapidated house — collecting dust, musk, and the smell of old, slowly forgotten happy memories mingled with the tragedy of their nonexistence.[4] There they were. And now they are gone. And that is a profoundly sad thing.

1. Loss of Childhood

"Where did all of that happiness go?"
"Where is my innocence?"
"Where is that little boy I once was?"

---

[2] "When you go to war as a boy you have a great illusion of immortality. Other people get killed; not you ... Then you are badly wounded the first time you lose that illusion, and you know it can happen to you." Ernest Hemingway, "Introduction," in *Men at War: The Best War Stories of All Time* (New York: Crown Publishers, 1942), xiii.

[3] Death "alters the landscape of our lives. Its seismic upheavals leave us bewildered and disoriented." Richard Rice, *Suffering and the Search for Meaning* (Downers Grove, IL: IVP Academic, 2014), 21.

[4] Israel often, when facing their own deaths and exiles and judgments and losses, reverted to "pre-creation" chaos language to describe their current chaos: "Jeremiah likens the judgment coming on Israel to a return to pre-creation chaos: to an earth *formless and empty* (Jer. 4:23; cf. Gen. 1:2)." Yes — formless and empty — one very bottomless path of grief. Robin Routledge, *Old Testament Theology: A Thematic Approach* (Downers Grove, IL: IVP Academic, 2008), 136.

"Where is the little girl, who is now lost and afraid?"

Kraft Macaroni and Cheese — that's my totem of childhood:
blue box, take me back. It was all real. And hiking in state parks, with
my parents, who were three, four times my size. You and I are different
people now — as different from our childhood selves as we are from the
children scurrying around at our feet today. But that *was* us. And having
forgotten ourselves is a loss at the center of much of our sadness. We can
drive cars and motorcycles now. And drink, and have sex. And we have
lost the ability to distinguish between *getting lost in life* and losing our
"selves" to the process of life. And indeed, whether by sin or tragedy, we
are losing both.[5]

2. Loss of Home

> Sitting on a couch ... with youthful parents.
> Curled up in your mom's arms.
> Counting the marks on our bedroom ceiling.
> Laying in the yard.

We are a wandering people. We may have lived in the same
apartment for over a year, but we do not belong. Not anywhere in
particular. Not with anyone in particular. Our childhood dealt us an
unbeatable hand — so unbeatable, that our third decade makes God
look like a shady dealer.[6] Where do we belong? We have to reach back
into our childhood for vocabulary, even to articulate what "home" is.
None of these swamps or creatures in the badlands of "modern life" in
which we've sunk our feet can do anything for us — only cheap mimicry,
masks that give us brief callbacks to something we can hardly admit

---

[5] "The greatest danger, that of losing one's own self, may pass off as quietly as if it were nothing;
every other loss, that of an arm, a leg, five dollars, a wife, etc., is sure to be noticed." Søren Kierkegaard,
The Sickness Unto Death, XIX: *A Christian Psychological Exposition for Upbuilding and
Awakening*, ed. and trans. Edna H. Hong and Howard V. Hong (Princeton, NJ: Princeton
University Press, 1941), 49.
[6] "Once our youth, our childhood home, our loved ones are gone, there is no going back.
Irreversibility is a kind of death in the midst of life." Tim Keller, *Walking With God through Pain
and Suffering* (New York: Dutton, 2013), 46.

we've ever needed or lost.[7]

3. Loss of a Parent

> "They're … gone."
> "I'll never see them again."
> "It's hard to imagine life without them."

I wish I could remember what my dad's hands looked like — whether they looked younger or older, or whether they were vascular. I remember they were always warm, and seemed to swallow mine, like our hands fit perfectly together. I wish I could see his face again. I have a picture of him on my Desktop, which I chronically cover up with .docx icons. I wish I could *hug* him again. But all that he is — his sharpness, his youthful eyes, his giddy smile, his contagious laugh, his beer belly (which he was always trying to lose), his brown hair (which had turned from blonde as a child) — it's all burnt to a crisp, ash in the ground. But … I would do anything to see his hands again.

The loss of a parent leaves us half-orphaned; the loss of both renders us destitute. Do we fear anything more than losing the one to whom we belong?[8]

4. Loss of Love

> "We were supposed to be forever."
> "But, you promised."
> "But, I trusted you."

---

[7] "Life hurts more than death will. The hurt is not merely bodily, but mental and emotional. It is a hurt of the spirit. . . . It is a sense of being lost, abandoned, wandering. The signposts have all disappeared and there is no way of knowing where one is going. Or—to change the image—one is frozen in a place of pain and there is no way out of it." John Goldingay, *Old Testament Theology: Israel's Faith* (Downers Grove, IL: IVP Academic, 2006), 636.

[8] "Like bread, meat loaf, plate, and other stuff around me that had been left behind, I, too, had been left behind. I no longer 'belonged' to anyone in the unique way that a child forever belongs to his or her parents." Alexander Levy, *The Orphaned Adult: Understanding and Coping with Grief and Change After the Death of Our Parents* (New York: Perseus, 1999), 46. The notion of being "orphaned" as an adult is a powerful metaphor, and is gaining popularity in grief theory: When both parents die, "it is then that the adult child passes through the transition from son/daughter to 'orphan.'" Helen Marshall, "Midlife Loss of Parents: The Transition from Adult Child to Orphan," *Ageing International* 29, no. 4 (2004) 352 [351-367].

Once, she was my future wife — my love, my dream, my everything. Now, she's just an undeleted phone number — "Somebody That I Used To Know." Mathematically, it just doesn't make sense. "I went to the gym." "I told the jokes." "I made the promises." "I met the parents." One text, one coffee — it's all over; the driving, the flying, the "I love you's", reduced to penny stock. Weeks, months, years of being more important than school, friends, and work, gone. Feels like a scam. Lost love makes all love feel like a scam. And we grieve.

5. Loss of Community

"I'm alone."
"I used to be safe; now I'm on my own."
"People are scarier now, with sharper teeth."

How long has it been since you had close friends, who knew you so intimately that you felt loved, even without them having to say it? For many of us, it's been a while. I never felt more depressed and alone than the summer after I graduated from college. I went from "Paul the Senior" to "Never Heard of Him." That's all our twenties are. About three or four cycles of starting *completely from scratch*. That's a long time not to feel known. It's an eternity when every tool to forget our aloneness is available to us. We would forget our sadness, if it weren't so powerful. But the power of our grief certainly won't stop us from trying to avoid eye contact with our aloneness. Friends across the country, family moving on, surrounded by those who were closest to us getting married — the evidence for our forsakenness outweighs all other voices.

God and Our Grief

We are not necessarily seeking "relief" here. Perhaps we are. And perhaps we're not. In the wake of death, we can feel like "disoriented, half-dead flies."[9] Our affection for what is lost "trickles on in impotence, unconsciously, laboriously, towards a new creation that does not yet even exist."[10] Paul says, "But we do not want you to be uninformed, brothers, about those who are asleep, that you may not grieve as others do who have no hope" (1 Thessalonians 4:13). What does that mean? There is certainly no uniform Christian response to death.[11] Yet, God still shows up in the context of loss, skewing the dark, bringing fresh air into the smog. God gives five gifts to those facing loss:

1. Recollection

"It is important to remember what is important."

God is deeply nostalgic. He remembers our personal stories; he sees the spider-web that composes the symphony of joy and pain that we experience. Why do you think the first *nine* chapters of Chronicles are simply lists of names and possessions? Because God is there in those moments — he loves taking polaroids of his beloved and including them in his word, in our remembering. We gloss over them, because we didn't know them.

But God prepares us for the death of Saul in 1 Chronicles 10 with nine chapters of recollection, of childhoods, of celebrations, of marriages, of new births, of aspirations and fulfillments, and deteriorations — lives, full and short — and then Saul: "The LORD put him to death and turned the kingdom over to David" (1 Chron 10:14).

---

[9] Hans Urs von Balthasar, *You Crown the Year with Your Goodness: Sermons through the Liturgical Year*, trans. Graham Harrison (San Francisco: Ignatius Press, 1989), 87. John Calvin used the exact same language, when he learned of the death of his refugee friend Claude Féray and the son of the recipient of the letter, victims of the plague: "When I received the message about the death of master Claude and of your son Louis, I was so shocked and so despondent that for several days I could only cry. And although I tried to find strength in the presence of God and wanted to comfort myself with the refuge he grants us in time of need, I still felt as if I was not at all myself. Really, I was no longer able to do the normal things, as if I myself were half dead." John Calvin, "To Monsieur de Richebourg, April 1541," *Letters of John Calvin: Compiled from the Original Manuscripts and Edited with Historical Notes*, 4 vols., trans. David Constable, ed. Jules Bonnet (Edinburgh: Thomas Constable and Co., 1885), 222 [222-229].

[10] Hans Urs von Balthasar, *Heart of the World*, trans. Erasmo Laiva (San Francisco: Ignatius, 1979), 152.

[11] "No mater how much thought goes into our attempts to interpret the experience, a life-changing loss never makes perfect sense. There are always facets of the experience that defy comprehension." Richard Rice, *Suffering and the Search for Meaning* (Downers Grove, IL: IVP Academic, 2014), 24.

"The Death of Saul and His Sons," the heading reads. That's very, very sad. But the LORD remembers his history with us, the good and the bad, even when we forget him. That's the greatest challenge of the grieving: to remember the good and the bad. When we are consumed with our sadness, it is often an overwhelming sense of the happiness or the tragedy. Both are real, and both are cherished by God.

Remembering *rightly* is hard. We can think of all the best, and feel sad that they are gone; or all the worst, and feel guilty that we weren't better. God calls that "lament," and invites us into all kinds of recollection — complaint, remembrance of joy, commemoration of honor, retelling of beautiful little moments. It is unbearable to us, dominated by our genre-specific faith, insisting on an epistolary resolution to our pain.

Let us join God in remembering our losses with pause and balance.

2. Rediscovery

"I have lost something that
used to make me *me*.
God, what is it?"

After Saul, David connected his spirituality with a sense of nostalgia from his younger self: "[The LORD] satisfies you with good so that your youth is renewed" (Psalm 103:5). We re-access the first-person of our youth — and we return again to our older, emerging selves through the lens of our childhood. In this, we find it easy to resort to simple, agricultural language once again "Man, his days are like grass; he flourishes like a flower of the field." (Psalm 103:5, 15)

Nostalgia is a compound of the Greek words: νόστος (nóstos), which means "return" or "homecoming," and ἄλγος (álgos), meaning "grief" or "pain." The emotion signifies a divided self – the heart experiences its unique at-home feeling, but the self also experiences the pangs of longing for the source. The source is the past, forever out of reach — "Let the little children come to me and do not hinder them, for to such belongs the kingdom of heaven" (Matthew 19:14).

Nostalgia reduces us to our lowest common denominator – it connects who we were in, perhaps, a simpler time to who we are as a distracted and divided person – "so that your youth is renewed," as David prayed. To enter into the past allows us to access who we used to be —uncomplicated, younger, louder — and assure ourselves, "I'm still that person. I haven't lost myself." This has been going on for ages. God has been doing this in his grieving children for ages — renewing their youth. He wants you to take the imaginary picture of your childhood self out of your wallet, and find yourself there — there, the place where the LORD satisfied you with good, the place where we find the embrace of Jesus easy, the place where we had not seen our love massacred by loss.

3. Resurrection

"One day, all loss will be overcome with life."

A future. We roll our eyes at "the afterlife" — no doubt, its irrelevance is flaunted in its entrance: death. But on the day we are raised with Christ, all our yearnings for home, all our longings for reconciliation and memories of our mother's arms, they will not be wiped away. We will not be turned into robots when we are made glorious with Christ: "So is it with the resurrection of the dead. What is sown is perishable; what is raised is imperishable" (1 Cor. 15:42). What we have known imperfectly, we will enjoy perfectly.

We don't like this comfort because it doesn't guarantee anything for us today. If our resurrection is God's throwing all of our earthly memories in a trash can for the sake of glory, our resurrection would be a tragedy. It would be a forgetting. Heaven would be a loss. But God's resurrection is not a white-washing of our most intimate memories — a bleaching of our deepest grief on earth. God's resurrection is a help to our grief:

"The hope of reunion on the other side of the grave is completely natural, genuinely human, and also in keeping with Scripture. For Scripture teaches us not a naked immortality of spectral souls but the eternal life of individual persons. Regeneration does not erase individuality, personality, or character, but sanctifies it and puts it to service in God's name."[12]

---

[12] Herman Bavinck, *Reformed Dogmatics, Volume 4: Holy Spirit, Church, and New Creation*, trans. John Vriend, ed. John Bolt (Grand Rapids, MI: Baker Academic, 2008), 640.

4. Reblossoming

"God, part of me has died.
Grow something new in its place."

Our bodies rarely heal "fully."[13] Shouldn't we expect the same from our hearts? We often speak of "healing" as though we can re-enter a world in which our loss is not real.[14] More often, a loss is definitive and irrevocable. What we wait for, then, with grief, is not a return to life before loss, but a blossoming of something new.

It's easy to feel guilty for "moving on" from something as good as our childhood, our home, our parent, our ex, our friends. Instead, we must imagine a time travel scenario in which we ask them face-to-face: "What do you want for me?" What does childhood you want for you? What did your mom or dad want for you? What did your friends want for you? A sense of meaning and joy, without a doubt. To be loved. To *receive* that love. Not to forget, no. But to live. Never new, but healing — in the truest sense.

If you can find the peace you once had, find it. But you may simply need to wait for your heart to grow something new. The loss I have experienced has felt more like laceration than loss. It makes sense why the West has popularized to the word "trauma" to speak not merely of massive horror, but of the common tragedies
we all face: because loss feels like our arm has been lopped off. Life moving forward may look more like waiting for God to grow something new, than fabricating a sense of being "over it."

---

[13] "Though he [Frodo] had been healed in Rivendell of the knife-stroke, that grim wound had not been without effect. His senses were sharper and more aware of things that could not be seen. One sign of change that he soon had noticed was that he could see more in the dark than any of his companions. . . . He felt the certainty of evil ahead and of evil following; but he said nothing. He gripped tighter on the hilt of his sword and went on doggedly." J. R. R. Tolkien, *The Fellowship of the Ring* (New York: Mariner, 1954), 304-305.

[14] This is evidenced by the fact that Good Friday services are often more populated than Easter Sunday: "Its tacit justification seems to be that Easter Sunday signals a victory so complete that God effectively annihilated Golgotha. Such confusion makes for a theology that is not merely bad, but heartless and even dangerous. . . . and dares to attempt what even God refused: obliterating the wounds of Christ Crucified." C. Clifton Black, "The Persistence of Wounds," in *Lament: Reclaiming Practices in Pulpit, Pew, and Public Square* (Louisville, KY: Westminster John Knox, 2005), 56 [47-58].

5. Resilience

"Help me to keep moving forward."

The pressure to bounce back from grief — to *get on* with life —
is the
common knee-jerk reaction.[15] There are certain allowances, but
persistent grief over loss seems to be frowned upon as a spiritual
weakness, a psychological deficit.[16] Grief is a barrier to health. An
obstacle to normalcy. But without the call to resilience in the face of
grief, the sadness of loss become shackles for us.

David lost two sons in his lifetime.[17]

---

[15] The temptation "is to find always the justification of the present in the future." And yet, "the Cross utterly prevents such a trivializing of the past." Donald MacKinnon, "Prayer, Worship, and Life," in *Philosophy and the Burden of Theological Honesty: A Donald MacKinnon Reader*, ed. John McDowell, T&T Clark Theology (New York: T&T Clark, 2011), 59 [55-66]. Nicholas Lash likewise insists: "The dark facticity of particular deeds and particular tragedy may not be obliterated for the sake of the coherence of the narrative." Nicholas Lash, "Ideology, Metaphor, and Analogy," in *Why Narrative?: Readings in Narrative Theology* (Eugene, OR: Wipf & Stock, 1997), 121 [113-137].

[16] Cato the younger, a 1st century B.C. Stoic philosopher and military commander, believed grief was an impurity, a weakness that only the unthoughtful suffer. And then his brother died, and his life was changed, and he spent wilds amount of money on the funeral of his brother, giving himself over to grief completely. "On this occasion, Cato forgot the philosopher, and testified the most pungent sorrow." William A. Becket, *A Universal Biography*, 3 vols. (London: w. Lewis, Finch-Lane, 1836), 707. "The Philosopher" is Cato's grandfather, Cato the elder, a prominent stoic philosopher who "argues that death is not an evil." Marcia L. Colish, *The Stoic Tradition from Antiquity to the Early Middle Ages, Volume I: Stoicism in Classical Latin Literature* (Leiden: Brill, 1985), 133. Rob Goodman and Jimmy Soni comment: "Cato gave himself to grief, this once, with the same fervor that had led him to preach the effeminacy of grief, the need for independence from pain in all things. For the rest of his life, friends and enemies alike would remark that this was the moment when philosophy most abandoned Cato." *Rome's Last Citizen: The Life and Legacy of Cato, Mortal Enemy of Caesar* (New York: Thomas Dunne Books, 2012), 56.

[17] Nicholas Wolterstorff, a Christian theologian, reflects on the death of his own son: "I have no explanation. I can do nothing else than endure in the face of this deepest and most painful of mysteries. I believe in God the Father Almighty, maker of heaven and earth and resurrecter of Jesus Christ. I also believe that my son's life was cut off in its prime. I cannot fit these pieces together. I am at a loss. I have read the theodicies produced to justify the ways of God to man. I find them unconvincing. To the most agonized question I have ever asked I do not know the answer. I do not know why God would watch him fall. I do not know why God would watch me wounded. I cannot even guess." Nicholas Wolterstorff, *Lament for a Son* (Grand Rapids, MI: Eerdmans, 1987), 67-68.

An infant:

"'Who knows whether the LORD
will be gracious to me, and the child may live?'
But now he is dead. . . . I shall go to him,
but he will not return to me."
(2 Sam. 12:22-23)

Then David arose from the earth ...
they set food before him,
and he ate.
(2 Sam. 12:20)

An adult:

"'O my son Absalom, my son,
my son Absalom!
Would I had died instead of you,
O Absalom, my son, my son!' ...
Then the king arose and took his seat in the gate."
(2 Sam. 18:33).

We mourn. No, that word is too indifferent. We blame, or cry, or get angry, or feel numb, or deny. And eventually, with our wounds, we take another step forward. We accept; we arise, and sit at in the common area of our lives, fulfilling our responsibilities, reclaiming all the artifacts of our past life in light of our new loss: staplers, commutes, contact information, voicemails, clothes, emotions, our relics from a time when we had what we no longer have. Our sadness is slow, or fast. Grief is tiring — so tiring that, at times, we are tempted to simply pitch our tent there until we die.

"It seemed to me a wearisome task, until I went into the sanctuary of God; then I discerned their end." (Psalm 73:16-17) If we resign ourselves to the weariness of grief forever, it will capture us in its clutches. "My flesh and my heart may fail, but God is the strength of my heart and my portion forever." (Psalm 73:26) David isn't dragging the dead body of his loss with the brute strength of his prayer life. It's easy to think that's what God wants us to do. No. David's heart fails, too. He fails. As J. I. Packer notes about grief: "We are all bad at it."[18]

Conclusion

That feeling you have — teeth against the pavement, skin rosy with blood, every piece of you rattling, not even close to holding it together — those are the spaces God enters. Those are the moments God kept me from certain suicide. Every year, my grief becomes more intense, because I allow myself to go a little deeper. I think about my dad: "The only country, known or unknown that I can breathe in, or care to, is the country in which we breathe together."[19] I long for that country. And whether I admit it or not, it is God's acting in my life to sustain me that allows me to wake up every day and do it all over again — feels like climbing Everest.

We have to resist latching onto promises that aren't true. It's tempting, when we hear assurances about the future, and about our pain, to hang on to them for a sense of meaning. But God doesn't promise us any earthly thing in this life. He is with us, and promises us many things about himself. But he is never cruel enough to tell us something untrue just to make us feel better.

One of the things God does for us is this: He gives us strength. "But I feel *so weak.*" Yet, whatever strength you *do* have … it is from him. Don't believe that your weakness is a sign of God's absence. Quite the opposite: your strength is a sign of his presence. Don't hold your grieving self to the standard of your "recovered" self. Look at the basic facts: you're conscious, breathing, vertical. There he is, doing his work. He is in the rowboat with you, in the fog, with no compass. But he is with you, facing real life by your side, hand around your shoulder:

---

[18] J. I. Packer, *A Grief Sanctified: Through Sorrow to Eternal Hope* (Wheaton, IL: Crossway, 2002),10.

[19] Tennessee Williams, *Camino Real* (New York: New Directions, 1953), 71. Take this alongside a later line: "But this is a port of entry and departure. There are no permanent guests." Ibid., 73.

This is the world; the lying likeness of
Our strips of stuff that tatter as we move
Loving and being loth;
The dream that kicks the buried from their sack
And lets their trash be honoured as the quick.
This is the world. Have faith.[20]

[20] Dylan Thomas, "Our Eunuch Dreams," *The Poems of Dylan Thomas: New Revised Edition* (New York: New Directions Publishing, 2003), 85 [84-85].

Chapter 10
Regret

"Become the voice of our forgotten places.
Teach us the names of what we have destroyed."[1]
    —Dana Gioia

Our twenties is the first decade in which we *really own* our decisions. When I was four, my dad would let me sit on his lap with my hands on the steering wheel. Life is kind of like that until our third decade. Most of the adolescent mistakes we make are frenzied and hyperventilated, but they don't pulverize the future. One day, we're used to conning our way in and out the cracks of pleasure, of self-centeredness, of absent-mindedness. The next, we're standing at the altar to make, before the judge to unmake, over the casket to farewell, in front of the disciplinarian to apologize — into the mist of a future *without* _____ — and we feel the weight of it being our fault. Regret is the closest emotional synonym we have for the word "scar."

I hadn't spoken with my dad for a year, in 2013. There were a lot of fights before that year. He was divorced, and alone, and had a history of aggression and drinking. But he was my dad. And even into seminary, I looked up to him as rugged and wise and wisecracking; irreplaceable — a double of Jackie Gleason. He taught me everything about being a man, good and bad. Racquetball. Weights. Girls. "The Church."

When I was a kid, he would pick up my sister and I from our mom's house, load our stuff in the car, and a mile or two out, drop me off on the side of the road. I was just too much of a handful. The nights I did end up at his house were spent cleaning up after his drinking, or watching he and my mom fight as she tried to rescue her children from

---

[1] Dana Gioia, "A California Requiem," *99 Poems: New & Selected* (Minneapolis, MN: Graywolf, 2016), 44 [43-44]. I am indebted to my sister Amy for introducing me to the poetry of Gioia, who lends real aesthetic aid to us twentysomethings.

their father — a man nobody understood, including himself. A Christian counselor, hearing about our relationship from childhood, used the word "trauma," and suggested I end communication immediately. So I did.

A year later, he started popping up on my radar — a Facebook message, an email, a voicemail. His last email to me had the subject line: "Matthew 18:21 and 18:22." He wrote:

> Paul,
>
> I was wondering what you thought about this scripture. Also, let me know if I can help you in any way....miss you much.
>
> Love,
> Dad

The thing is, my dad often did help. A lot. But I thought: "Forgive him ... seventy-seven times." Uh huh. "Typical manipulation," I thought. Not falling for it this time. My response:

> "Please stop trying to contact me."

I couldn't see his emotions. I couldn't see his pain. I couldn't see his desperation. I only saw an "abusive" father who couldn't be reasoned with.

> OK, Paul...But could you just tell me what I did to make things this way and if there is any way I can make things right again? It is extremely hurtful to not have contact with you and [your sister] and I would do whatever necessary to make things good between us all....I am so sorry for any hurt that I caused you and [your sister] and would just like the chance to be forgiven for my mistakes.....
>
> Love you both more than anything!
>
> Dad

I never doubted his love. I doubted the integrity of how he played *my* love for him. Yet, this was so unlike him. He never apologized for anything. We would usually just wait for a few weeks to pass to resume our normal interaction. But not now. Now, he's apologizing. For the first time in my life, he owned his weakness. He acknowledged his regrets. He *let* himself regret his sins, his mistakes.

A few days later, when I was home in New York out of nowhere, he approached me in the gym. He had a similar plea. Armed with my counselor-endowed sense of victimhood, I took my first opportunity in twenty-five years to chew him out — to stomp on his neck when he was weak. I barked a rap list of recriminations against him in exchange for his decades of placing the blame on me. I landed a final blow: "I hope you die of a heart attack."

Three days later, he died of an overdose of alcohol and oxycodone.

...

So ... regret. A grown man faces down the devil inside, and his son welcomes a newborn demon into the world. What do we do when, for the first time in our lives, God does not give us a second chance?

Five Aspects of Regret

As with any concept, to face it, we must begin with a clear definition. For our purposes, we will define regret this way:

> ## Definition:
>
> *Regret is the urgent desire to travel back in time in order to take back our action (or inaction), and the emotional fallout of being unable to do so.*

Of course, we Mad Lib that definition with lots of other emotions — disappointment, terror, guilt, grief, and more.[2] However, regret *proper* is simply the unquenchable thirst for what might have been. There is an entire field of psychological study called "might-have-been studies," which focuses on regret. And inside the container of what-might-have-been is full of our active heart's mushing through the snow of possibility — afraid of being stuck in a life we don't want, paranoid that we'll be caught (or devastated that we were), saddened by our hand in tragedy, uncertain of what to do with our own fault in our suffering, trapped by our responsibility. Regret is shape-shifting in that way.

Psychologists refer to regret as the engine that cycles us rapidly between depression and anxiety — the "amplifier of the repetitive thought-distress relationship."[3] There are at least five speakers attached to that amplifier.

1. Guilt

"I deserve the worst."
"Why did God even create me?"
"I could have prevented this if I had been better."
"I could have stopped this if I had *done* better."
"It's always my fault."

---

[2] Various dictionaries have used the term "disappointment" in the *very definition* of regret. But this doesn't comport with science. The two are, while closely related, entirely different emotions. Significant differences emerged between disappointment and regret in one study: "These differences were most pronounced for 'action tendencies' (what participants felt like doing) and 'emotivations' (what they were motivated to do). These results suggest that the two emotions have differential implications for future behavior." Marcel Zeelenberg, Wilco W. van Dijk, Antony S. R. Manstead, and Joop van der Pligt, "The Experience of Regret and Disappointment," *Cognition and Emotion* 12, no. 2 (1998): 221-230.

[3] Neal J. Roese, Kai Epstude, Florian Fessel, Adam D. Galinsky, Mike Morrison, Rachel Smallman, Suzanne Segerstrom, and Amy Summerville, "Repetitive Regret, Depression, and Anxiety: Findings From a National Survey," *Journal of Social and Clinical Psychology* 28, no. 6 (2009): 685 [671-688].

I live in a studio apartment next to a college football field. I routinely find myself in the bleachers, hunched over, sobbing "I'm sorry," hoping my dad can hear me.[4] Life is good when we have, at the very least, our high horse to take us away from the sting of our suffering. But regret stares us in the face when we have betrayed the horse. We are not *trained* for when life trades in our circumstances for consequences. But this won't last for long. Guilt always leads to repression. Guilt is like a chili pepper, flavoring everything, not subtle, unfixable, except with time. That's why our guilt in regret feels more like cancer than an execution. The more we deny it, the more it takes ownership of our frantic reactions; the more we accept it, the more it consumes our emotions.

2. Grief

"I'll never get a chance to undo this."
"She was the one that got away."
"It wasn't supposed to be this way."
"It's not fair."
"It's going to feel this way forever."

When we regret, we are faced with a lost future. *The option* to change made reality palatable.[5] Now, our options have abandoned us. Love is lost, opportunity disappeared, respectability mottled, and reputation splintered in the wood chipper of our wrong-choosing. We wish we had spent more time with them, or less; that we had been less cautious with them, or more. Whatever the case, life drags us on, further and further from our loss, with a piece of its skull lodged in our chest. Whatever died, it is part of us forever.

3. Humiliation

"I'm ruined. Forever."

---

[4] Nobel Prize winner Daniel Kahneman explains: "Regret is an emotion, and it is also a punishment that we administer to ourselves." Daniel Kahneman, *Thinking, Fast and Slow* (New York: Farrar, Straus and Giroux), 346.
[5] "People's biggest regrets are a reflection of where in life they see their largest opportunities; that is, where they see tangible prospects for change, growth, and renewal. Neal J. Roese and Amy Summerville, "What We Regret Most ... and Why," *Personality and Social Psychology Bulletin* 31, no. 9 (2005): 1273 [1273-1285].

"What have I done…"
"People will think I'm such an idiot."
"People see me as dirty, disgusting."

Our indignity is exposed. Whatever we have done, it was the wrong choice — we are "discovered unmasked … blushing."[6] We line up all the variables, we solve for X, and … the conclusion is inescapable: we *need* to fix this. The problem is us. We run our nails through the possibilities — is there *any* way to undo this? We feel that the only solution is "to magically expunge something which was actually done."[7] We know the *ending* of the book of Job — God comes down and gives him a new family — but we feel a little more at home in chapter 3: "Let the day perish on which I was born, and the night that said, 'A man is conceived'" (Job 3:3).

4. Fear

"I will *never* go through this again."
"I won't make the same mistake twice."
"I'm never letting this happen again."

Regret — our arms drop limp at our sides; but we clench our shield and hold it tight. We hedge our bets. Pain is always scary. But the *fear* of regret is starvation for our ambitions, and steroids for our inhibitions. We're conquered by the fear of missing out.[8] There is not a more agonizing thought that your current life is not "Your Best Life Now." Worse than that — regret says, "Your 'Best Life' isn't even possible anymore." "Your best spouse…" "Your best job…" "Your happiest situation…" "Gone." That makes us nauseous.

---

[6] Westermann, *Genesis 1-11* (Minneapolis: Augsburg, 1974), 236.
[7] Janet Landman, "Regret: A Theoretical and Conceptual Analysis," *Journal for the theory of Social Behavior* 17, no. 2 (1987): 146 [135-160].
[8] On the science of "FOMO" — "Actions, or errors of commission, generate more regret in the short term; but inactions, errors of omission, produce more regret in the long run." Thomas Gilovich and Valeria H. Medvec, "The Experience of Regret: What, When, and Why," *Psychological Review* 102, no. 2 (1995): 379 [379-395]. Again, from Ruth M. J. Byrne: "the imagined outcome is better than the actual one for the inaction but not for the action. … People regret inactions because they can imagine a better outcome." Ruth M. J. Byrne, *The Rational Imagination: How People Create Alternatives to Reality* (Cambridge, MA: Massachusetts Institute of Technology, 2005), 61.

We regret getting married. Ugh. We hear about it all the time — waking up to someone the day after the wedding, with the sinking feeling of being stuck for the next 60 years. Is there any thing worse? Here, imagination works against us in two ways: (1) the intensity of our regret is based solely on how *good* we can imagine our life might have been, and (2) the intensity of our *fear* of regret is based on how miserable we imagine we'd be on the wrong path.[9] In a nutshell: there is nothing I wouldn't do to avoid having a second-best situation (or avoid experiencing a painful situation *again*, like heartbreak).

5. A Closed Universe

"There's no way back…"
"God, why didn't you stop this?"
"Please … is there any chance we can fix this?"
"Why did you let me do this?"

We no longer have the world ahead of us. We've traded an open future for a closed hallway, ever-narrowing. The key symptom here is repetition: playing in our heads over and over and over again. Rehashing, re-running the simulation, wishing ourselves back five minutes, five years.

One study found that, while grief, guilt, and self-blame all decline over time, regret is the one emotion that persists at the same level of intensity over one's lifetime.[10] Maybe that's because age persuades us to give up our dreams of time travel, which leaves us in a hopeless place. Yes, theologies have emerged in history to make room for "praying for things not to have happened."[11] I get that. But I also know that it is impossible. We live in a closed universe, a closed hull of a sinking ship, capsized with a single cannonball.

---

[9] Janet Landman comments: "Regret then may depend … simply on how imaginative one is." Janet Landman, "Regret: A Theoretical and Conceptual Analysis," *Journal for the Theory of Social Behavior* 17, no. 2 (1987): 154 [135-160].

[10] Margaret Stroebe, Wolfgang Stroebe, Rens van de Schoot, Henk Schut, Georgios Abakoumkin, Jei Li, "Guilt in Bereavement: The Role of Self-Blame and Regret in Coping with Loss," *PLOSone* 9, no. 5 (2014), 1-9.

[11] See Thomas P. Flint, "Praying for Things to Have Happened," *Divine Providence: The Molinist Account*, Cornell Studies in the Philosophy of Religion (Ithica, NY: Cornell University Press, 1998), 229-250.

God and Our Regret

Regret is a mark of human life: "because it distinguishes us from other species, regret is intrinsically human."[12] Obviously, if we could live lives that didn't require time travel, that would be ideal: "Though we would like to live without regrets, and sometimes proudly insist that we have none, this is not really possible, if only because we are mortal."[13]

I can't promise you more than what my dad received — dying alone, rejected by his wife and children. But there is hope in this life for those who trust God. It's scary to trust God without guarantees. I met with the pastor who counseled my dad before he died. That pastor counseled me for an hour. That pastor offered me nothing more than he offered my dad. And in that moment, I realized, sitting in the same chair in which my dad had sat in despair, that the embrace of Christ was all either of us were ever looking for. And, while death had taken my dad — unbeliever or not — God had kept me on earth. There were days I wanted to die, because I didn't want to live a life with my dad's death hanging over my head. And yet, the tragedy of regret means something profoundly different for those living than those dead. Here are five ways that God redirects our desire to take back the past:

1. Repurposement

"I can use this."

For all the truth that regret speaks, it speaks a false word of prophecy about your end — *nothing* is certain about what can happen. Did you cannibalize a loving relationship that cannot be reversed? Did you commit a sin that has been recognized and punished? Were you caught in the act? Were you negligent? Were you obsessive? Yes, unlike depression and anxiety and self-blame, regret's hand on your shoulder remains truthfully sober and steady over time.

---

[12] Marcel Zeelenberg and Rik Pieters, "A Theory of Regret Regulation 1.0," *Journal of Consumer Psychology* 17. No. 1 (2007): 15 [3-18].
[13] James Baldwin, "God's Country," *The New York Review of Books* 8 (March 23, 1967): 20.

Why couldn't God have changed it? Why couldn't God have prevented you? What would we tell our childhood selves? What year would we travel to? Why couldn't J. J. Abrams have written my life instead of God? As closed as our universe is, don't let regret convince you that it *knows* your future. Look at these four instances of regret in Scripture:

"Then all the congregation lifted up their voices and cried, and the people wept that night. ... 'Would that we had died in the land of Egypt! Or would that we had died in this wilderness!'" (Num. 14:1-2). Whoops. Shouldn't have trusted God there.

"When Judas ... saw that Jesus was condemned, he changed his mind" (Matthew 27:3). Yikes. Should've trusted God there.

"Immediately a rooster crowed a second time. And Peter remembered how Jesus had made the remark to him, 'Before a rooster crows twice, you will deny Me three times.' And he began to weep." (Mark 14:72) Okay ... maybe God's up to something.

"For even if I made you grieve with my letter, I do not regret it— though I did regret it, for I see that that letter grieved you, though only for a while. As it is, I rejoice, not because you were grieved, but because you were grieved into repenting." (2 Cor. 7:8)[14]

---

[14] Paul even regretted writing a letter (though only for a while) that produced repentance! The letter he regretted (though only for a while) is not 1 Corinthians, but a "severe letter," likely as a result of wrongdoing done to Paul while in Corinth. See Paul Barnett, *The Second Epistle to the Corinthians*, The New International Commentary on the New Testament (Grand Rapids, MI: Eerdmans, 1997), 372-275.

Don't believe the word regret has spoken over you. You can't change the past, but don't let regret convince you of a future that doesn't exist yet. We'll find ourselves regretting right in the middle of God's plan. And we'll find ourselves regretting our real sin. In both cases, God is redeeming and moving and creating a future. You may be *very certain* about your past, but *you don't know your future* — what others will bring love and healing into your life, what ways God will breathe new meaning into your exasperated lungs, what new hope may bud.

Hope for hope. Our regrets can germinate a new future for under the ashen trees of the lives which we have burnt to the ground. "The Lord is faithful. He will establish you and guard you against the evil one" (2 Thessalonians 3:3). A promise to non-regretters and regretters alike — in fact, our regretful patterns are what makes God's faithful patterns at all necessary for us.

2. Repentance

"I repent." — "Enough said."

The greatest barrier to repentance is our fear of regretting *missing out* on
the sin, as if a life with missed opportunities for pleasure is a lesser life — the fear of regret keeps us bound in regretful patterns. We have many paths to process regret — morbid reflection, suppression, attempting to undo the act, avoiding the consequences of the act, and, perhaps when we are through with these, the productive path: repentance.

> "Godly grief produces a repentance that leads to salvation without regret, whereas worldly grief produces death."
> (2 Corinthians 7:8-10)

Everybody who gets drunk has a hangover. Regret over consequences is no safeguard against future regret. It's easy to convince ourselves that *feeling badly* counts as our penance for an act — where both "counts" and "penance" are errors in understanding. Paul was slaving to make a point to the Corinthians in a way they could hear: "Continuance in unrepentance, characterized by nothing more than shallow remorse unaccompanied by positive action ... could have ... led, in time, to their spiritual 'death.'"[15]

Whatever our reason for regret, whether it is right or not, whether it's holy or sinful, it yanks our eyes inward and says, "Avoid death. That felt very much like death. Don't do that again." It's a creational prompt toward a redemptive reality: "Therefore repent." (Rev. 2:16) We don't want to repent. We want a *do over*. Some of us might get one. Some of us might not. The most immediate gift God gives the regretful is the call to repent. It may not take us back in time, but it may heal some wounds, and prevent some more. Let's exchange our regret-inducing patterns "for all endurance and patience with joy" (Colossians 1:11).

3. Reckless Abandon

"Let's keep risking."

"Wisdom" has become Christian code for "cautionary." Sometimes, it is great wisdom to take a great risk—to "sell everything .... and buy that field" (Matthew 13:44). God is not beyond regret. Why? Because regret can simply be the correct response to the *negative consequences* of the right choice:

"And the LORD regretted that he had made man on the earth, and it grieved him to his heart." (Genesis 6:6)

"The word of the LORD came to Samuel: 'I regret that I have made Saul king, for he has turned back from following me and has not performed my commandments.' And Samuel was angry, and he cried to the LORD all night." (1 Samuel 15:10-11)

Did God know that man would sin against him, and that Saul would disobey? Yes. But he ordained it anyway. And he wouldn't take it back.

---

[15] "Continuance in unrepentance, characterized by nothing more than shallow remorse unaccompanied by positive action ... could have ... led, in time, to their spiritual 'death.'" Barnett, *Second Corinthians*, 377.

"And also the Glory of Israel will not lie or have regret, for he is not a man, that he should have regret." (1 Samuel 15:29)

Regret — the feeling that consumes us when we feel the negative consequences of our actions — doesn't keep God from diving headfirst into the world. We think that if we were God — especially if we were the *real,* living God — we wouldn't have any regrets. That's true, in the sense of "No purpose of yours can be thwarted" (Job 42:2). But it's *not* true in the sense that God enters into a world which has *real risk,* and he deliberately and sovereignly enters into a world full of regrets. He dignifies our worthy regrets. He legitimizes our *risks.* He critiques our "anticipatory regret" with his exposed grief, held in the heart of his unwavering
control.

If you have regrets, you're in good company. "I see it all perfectly; there are two possible situations—one can either do this or that. My honest opinion and my friendly advice is this: do it or do not do it—you will regret both."[16] Don't let regret stop you from loving, from feeling, from engaging, from protecting. Life comes to an end, and in our short years on earth, we will regret putting off worthy risks more than anything.[17] "There is no later. This is later."[18]

Don't let anyone tell you that true Christianity requires a riskless life. Step into risk, don't hedge your bets, and own your decisions. Regret can be a positive gift,[19] not least in the way it gives us access to the regretful heart of God, as he faces negative consequences because of love. God knows that after all the wounds humanity deals him, at the end, he will be "a Lamb standing, as though it had been slain" (Rev 5:6), and we will be with him. God wills the negative consequences of his own good

---

[16] Søren Kierkegaard, *Either/Or* (1842), in *A Kierkegaard Anthology,* ed. R. Bretall (Princeton, NJ: Princeton University Press, 1946)
[17] "This very evening is the real time of our life." Alexander Schmemann, *For the Life of the World: Sacraments and Orthodoxy* (Crestwood, NY: St. Vladimir's Seminary Press, 2004), 62.
[18] Cormac McCarthy, *The Road* (New York: Vintage Books, 2006), 54.
[19] One study found that stepping into risk that we own, without tons of oversight, prompts the most amount of growth: "individuals are more likely to learn when they have responded to an event with upward-directed, self-focused counterfactual thoughts, and, additionally, that this learning process is inhibited by accountability to organizational superiors." Michael W. Morris and Paul C. Moore, "The Lessons We (Don't) Learn: Counterfactual Thinking and Organizational Accountability after a Close Call," *Administrative Science Quarterly* 45, no. 4 (2000): 737-765.

decisions, because he knows what glorious thing he will do with them in heaven. We can persevere with God through our own good risk, even though we don't know the exact end, except that we will stand with him in the last day, scars and all.

4. Revision

"Lesson learned. Moving on."

Jesus isn't a one trick pony. He isn't a cosmic garbage man that we need to keep taking our trash away from us. We don't need him merely to "heal" our regrets. Our theology shouldn't incline us always to assume that our negative emotions are things God wants to take away. Regret opens opportunity for revision: "Then Saul said, 'I have sinned. Return, my son David, for I will not harm you again because my life was precious in your sight this day. Behold, I have played the fool and have committed a serious error.'" (1 Sam 26:21) "That was dumb." Regret may leave us incapacitated and alone and hopeless … but in the weeds, we might catch a glimpse of an opportunity for improvement. Henry David Thoreau tells us: "Make the most of your regrets; never smother your sorrow, but tend and cherish it till it comes to have a separate and integral interest. To regret deeply is to live afresh."[20]

Live afresh, and pray for the Spirit to do in you what it did in that moment in the heart of Saul: "Behold." That's Saul's regret. Disgraced before those whom he has hurt. Sometimes, the shameless have a hard time with this step. But often, the regretful are stuck here. "I have played the fool." We loop our regrets on repeat. We know the intricacies of our folly. "And have committed a serious error." David responds to Saul by giving him back his spear — time for revision. "Then Saul said to David, 'Blessed be you, my son David! You will do many things and will succeed in them." (1 Sam 26:25) We know that Saul dies an unhappy death. But he processes his regret here in the right way. He recognizes, and he moves on to bless.

Try not to get stuck at any one of these steps — regret, replay, or recognition — always push your regret through to revision.

---

[20] Henry David Thoreau, "Nov. 13, 1839," *Autumn: From the Journal of Henry D. Thoreau*, ed. H. G. O. Blake (New York: Houghton, Mifflin and Company, 1900), 260.

5. Release

"It's over. It's okay.
We still have each other."

The last place the regretful will go is Scripture. Why would we go to a book that shames us? "Be holy, because I am holy" (1 Peter 1:16). The regretful are not a holy people. Or are they? Where would we fit in Scripture? It's obvious. *Out.* Out where? Probably "the blazing furnace, where there will be weeping and gnashing of teeth" (Matthew 13:42). Yes, there.[21]

Well, maybe not. Scripture doesn't cast us out. There are more fitting and redemptive roles to play for the regretful. God wrote regret into the script of redemptive history, and therefore the Christian life — it's part of the plan. For those who have sinned, God gives the words, "The Lord has forsaken me; my Lord has forgotten me" (Isaiah 49:14).

Okay, so there are words for the regretful, but are there any *positive* words? Yes. Look to the crucified criminal. Publicly displayed, without excuse, exiled, punished, regretful, naked, utterly ashamed, interjecting into Jesus's cry, "Remember me" (Luke 23:42).

The criminal is "crucified with Christ" (Galatians 2:20), who cries "Why have you forsaken me?" (Matthew 27:46). Christ enters into the experience of regret so that he can sit with us in the Holy Saturday that is this present age.

Jesus said to this thief, "Truly, I say to you, today you will be with me in Paradise." (Luke 23:43). This man did regretful things his entire life. He couldn't have felt it more than ever while hanging on a cross, facing his own death because of his regrets — possibly leaving children behind, leaving loved ones behind, leaving destruction in his wake. And yet, his regretful patterns brought him to the side of Jesus; to the fountain of eternal life.

Even if you never made *one* decision in your life that brought negative consequences, you would not be in control of your life. You would not be in control of the next moment. You would not be able to

---

[21] "Blame and guilt are special kinds of causal beliefs, and unfair aspersions cast on others, heartless blaming of victims, and needless self-blame are all the work of the dark side of counterfactual thinking." Neal Roese, *If Only: How to Turn Regret into Opportunity* (New York: Broadway Books, 2005), 85-86.

pour out all of your critical and ethical analysis before God to persuade him to change your fate. What will be will be. What God gives us is himself:

> "Our inability to reach one another, the inability of the mother to console her child who is suffering, the inability of friendship to prevent misunderstandings and divisions, the inability of love to prolong communion and to abolish distances, the loneliness in which we are locked up, the suffering of a tortured humanity— Jesus lives all this in his agony, not from the outside as if he were a saddened witness, but from the inside and in all the greatest depths, as the loneliest and most abandoned of all. From the depths of this loneliness, Jesus Christ can at last gather into unity the dispersed sons of God (Jn 11:52). . . . He can reach us all and reunite us."[22]

Conclusion

In this life, I'll never be able to look into my dad's eyes and say, "I'm sorry for pushing you away. I wish I could take it back. Will you forgive me?" And he'll never be able to look into mine and say, "It's okay." That's not depression. That's not guilt. That's regret. And there's absolutely nothing I can do to change *that* situation.

We need to journal. Pray. Relate. Get face-to-face with people who love us. Whether we need to feel relieved from regret, or have someone acknowledge the wrongness of what we did, we must figure out what we need, and seek it. Regret has a *long* shelf life. Sometimes we need to keep it on the shelf. And other times, we need God to help us figure out what to do with it.

Sometimes we need "It's not your fault." And other times we need to hear directly from God: "as far as the east is from the west, so far does he remove our transgressions from us." (Psalm 103:12)

Lord, have mercy on us, and all our regrets.

---

[22] Jacques Guillet, "Rejeté Des Hommes Et De Dieu," *Christus* 49, no. 13 (1966): 80-90 [83-100].

Chapter 11

Suicidality

I held it truth, with him who sings
To one clear harp in divers tones,
That men may rise on stepping-stones
Of their dead selves to higher things."[1]
—Sir, Alfred Lloyd Tennyson

Suicide is the one waiting at the end of the line, when I've failed wrangling all my "quarter life issues," who patiently waits for me when I'm exhausted, and trapped, and frantic.[2] My switching jobs, my feeling overwhelmed and lost, my confusing relationships, my nail-biting, my food-purging — suicide swims beneath the surface of all these realities, offering a knowing glance when I need it, signaling inevitable doom, patiently reiterating life's undeniable bleakness. And when suicide submits its proposal, it feels infallible and irresistible. Suicide knows that I'm tethered to him, and no matter how many mindfulness tricks I use to

---

[1] Sir Alfred Lloyd Tennyson, "In Memoriam A. H. H.," *The Works of Alfred Lord Tennyson*, Wordsworth Poetry Library (Hertfordshire: Wordsworth Editions Limited, 1994), 310.

[2] Most literature on suicide is on suicide *prevention*. But I will speak in the first person in the chapter, both because my experience allows me to, and because I hope to add to the small collection of writings in the universe that make eye contact with the content of suicide itself. Prevention is a worthy topic on which to have resources. Most of them are thorough and empirical and specific. But they tell us tediously obvious things, like the fact that suicide is associated with depression and hopelessness. But resources for sufferers themselves are scarce. And the few that do exist are so generic, because the causes for suicide are too disparate, cold and clinical. In fact, modern suicide prevention strategies that have risen over the past decade have done little to put a dent in the national suicide rate: "Despite significant developments in treatment research and increased use of health-care services among suicidal persons in the United States, there appears to have been little change in the rates of suicide or suicidal behavior over the past decade." (Matthew K. Nock, Guilherme Borges, Evelyn J. Bromet, Christine B. Cha, Ronald C. Kessler, and Sing Lee, "Suicide and Suicidal Behavior," *Epidemiologic Reviews* 30 (2008) 146 [133–154.) This chapter is an attempt to sing with the small choir of sufferers who lament their scattered and unequivalent intolerances. This isn't meant to be technical or clinical or preventative. This chapter is simply for people like me who need someone to not only take their ideations seriously, but their feelings and concerns as well.

escape his rope, the grey heaviness of life will sink my soul back down to him.

I have an awkward and intimate relationship with suicide.[3] He is a welcome suitor for me — a stalker who panders to my hidden feelings. He paints my pain with an arrow sign. He wipes my tears with a plan. He is the shining light at the bottom of the well — when I miss my mom, when I miss my childhood, when I hate school, when I'm rejected by a girl, when I feel like I don't belong, when I'm certain that God would take back his promises to me if he could. Surely he doesn't want another addict in the world.

Surely God wouldn't want another sexually dirty person walking the earth. Surely the bullies are God's prophets, angels of condemnation he has sent to mock the imperfect.

Suicide doesn't even need to speak; he can nod when the right words are spoken. He gestures to the same door, with a crescendo, over and over: "It would be so much easier." "You would be free from this pain." "Then *they* would be free from the pain you cause them." "Then they would feel bad about what they've done to you." "Then they would love you." "Then you would be with God (probably)."

It's easy to dramatize suicide. As soon as we hear the word, we imagine visions of being carted to the emergency room and strapping them down to a bed. But physical sedations and interventions don't combat suicide *per se*. Suicide is a power with suggestive force. Suicide draws from the power of legitimate pain. It expects to be dismissed through trite advice (too weak) or hospital threats (too strong), only strengthening its persuasion.

Suicidal temptations are muted cries. Those who feel the pull of suicide know that taking it seriously does not first mean arguing with it, but understanding it. Suicide has strength when we fear to look it in the eye. Its kryptonite is not always in pulling back from pain, but pushing into it. Suicide has several vulnerabilities. But beneath them all is a willingness to understand pain. Successful combatants are those who

---

[3] Hopefully that's a benefit to you. As suicide survivor Craig Miller put it: "The best way to speak to a suicidal heart is *with* a suicidal heart." Linda Matchan, "Suicide-Attempt Survivors Go Public in Hope of Aiding Many At Risk," *Boston Globe* April 29, 2014. https://www.bostonglobe.com/lifestyle/style/2014/04/28/suicide-attempt-survivors-speak-about-their-experiences-hoping-reach-those-risk/ffrjBg4qQPLHlvi9srqKBP/story.html. Accessed on July 25, 2016.

speak to their pain in a recognizable voice.

Five Aspects of Our Suicidality

Professionals who dabble in these deep waters put all of these voices in a box called *suicidal ideations* — thoughts, feelings, and behaviors inclining oneself toward self-killing (*sui*, of self; *cide*, murder). But we can parse the term a little bit more. *Parasuicide* is a generic aim at death, which fails. *Feigned suicide* is a genuine attempt to mimic and fail suicide, succeeding in life. There are also *non-fatal cosmic gambles* — weak intentioned gestures toward death, which may either fail or succeed. Here, in understanding these distinctions, we can define suicidality this way:[4]

> ## Definition:
>
> *A person is suicidal when they begin to see death as an actionable solution to their pain.*

I think my dad made a non-fatal cosmic gamble, with oxycodone and alcohol. I'll never know, of course.

I almost killed myself once. With my dad's gun, soon after he died. And there was a man who pulled me out of that place, when I

---

[4] Meyer et al., claim that "suicidality" is not a proper substitute for "suicidal ideation," yet this conclusion is for the purpose of surveilling the population for the suicidal, not for developing terminology of self-understanding,to which end I find the term "suicidality" a helpful term. "Suicidality and Risk of Suicide—Definition, Drug Safety Concerns, and a Necessary Target for Drug Development: A Brief Report," *Journal of Clinical Psychiatry* 71, no. 8 (2010): 1040-1046.

couldn't.[5] Here are a few voices that we become too tired to fight before long.

1. Hurt

"I can't keep living like this."

Someone once said: "What is forgotten is unavailable, and what is unavailable cannot be healed." Like an innocent shriek expresses happy surprise, and sobbing expresses sadness, suicide expresses a complex bundle of buried pain. If the soul is a building, each floor a layer of grief, sadness, anger, depression, and exhaustion, then suicidal ideations are the bat signal on top of everything — "help."[6]

I remember sitting with my mom on a couch in my empty apartment, unable to cry, unable to express anything except: "I don't know what to do. I know that if life keeps going on like this, I'm going to kill myself. I can't do it. I just can't." When she left, I cried.

In the moment, the pain feels unsearchable, divine, inerrant. It simply power washes the brain with the pain of a cracked femur, except there are no outward signs. A lost girlfriend. A lost scholarship. Heartache cries out: "Make it real. Make the pain real."[7] Suicide is an attempt to make available what is unavailable — it is a twisted shot to expose the monster, to reach out for healing. It is a wailing isolation. It is

---

[5] That puts me in company with 1.8 million other adults in the U.S. See Center for Disease Control, "Suicide: Facts At a Glance," (2015): access at http://www.cdc.gov/ViolencePrevention/pdf/Suicide-DataSheet-a.pdf. Male deaths represent 79% of all US suicides — that means that male suicides alone in 2013 (32,055) dwarf total suicides in 2001 (30,000) by 2,000. Male suicides are most commonly performed with a firearm (56.9% — how's that for masculinity?). Suicide is the fourteenth leading cause of death among females, the seventh leading cause of death among males, and *the third leading cause of death among persons 15–34 years old* (i.e., millennials). Ibid.

[6] "Intractable pain or unbearable mental anguish make life seem so miserable that death appears largely as a liberation, regardless of what expectation a person may have regarding the hereafter." Norman L. Farberow and Edwin Schneidman, *Cry for Help* (New York: McGraw-Hill, 1965), 195. *Cry for Help* was one of the first books to systematize this idea — that suicidal ideations are not simply inclinations of immorality or mental derangement, but contain their own legitimate emotional logic.

[7] "Lethality—the idea that 'I can stop this pain; I can kill myself'—is the unique essence of suicide." Edwin S. Schneidman, *The Suicidal Mind* (New York: Oxford University Press, 1996), 8.

a hurting cry for help.[8]

2. Depression

"My world is too dark to keep going."

The dull weight of depression can be crushing. It stirs unstoppable sadness in the cauldron of our souls, turning us inward toward our sadness, always facing our pain, always experiencing the world through the lens of our misery, blinding us to the good. This may seem like a direct cause of suicide, but it's not. It's a direct occasion for coping. Suicide doesn't sharpen its axe on sadness, but on failed coping mechanisms for that sadness.[9]

Depression is not *sadness*, as in grief or nostalgia.[10] Depression is sadness that has taken the operating seat, calling all the emotional shots, shutting down all regulatory protocols, leaving us defenseless, possessed by melancholy, our bodies like haunted houses. Like a drunk operating heavy machinery, depression is when sadness insists on being the topic of every thought, and insists on taking appropriate action. Depression has a tendency to dominate the emotional life with dreary obscurity, and force us to resolve its tensions at whatever cost.

3. Hopelessness

"There is no escape from this pain."

---

[8] Cutting carries the same logic: "Cutting is really a remarkable, ingenious solution to the problem of not existing. It provides concrete, irrefutable proof that one is alive." Marilee Strong, *A Bright Red Scream: Self-Mutilation and the Language of Pain* (New York: Penguin, 1998), 55. In a sense, then, self-mutilation is a last-ditch effort to fend one's soul from the clutches of non-existence — the same clutches which threaten to pull the last breath from their lungs through suicide.

[9] "Depression becomes a significant factor when … coping mechanisms begin to fail and their view of the world and of themselves becomes significantly negative." Ralph L. V. Rickgarn, *Perspectives on College Student Suicide*, Death, Value and Meaning Series (Amityville, NY: Baywood Publishing Company, 1994), 102.

[10] See Francis Mark Mondimore, M.D., *Depression: The Mood Disease*, 3rd ed. (Baltimore, MD: The Johns Hopkins University Press, 2006), 5.

Inscribed above the entrance to Dante's Hell is "Abandon every hope, all you who enter." And the visitor responds, "These words I see are cruel."[11] The suicidal heart is trapped in its misery, tortured by suffering's cruel persistence. Like a journal article with a thousand footnotes, the suicidal heart cites a thousand moments of unending pain to support one irrefutable thesis: the suffering will never end, and there is only one way to end it.

Concepts like "joy" and "heaven" and "God" and "gospel" exist on the other side of the bulletproof glass, with other people — better, more normal people. And no matter how much we pray or read the Bible or go to counseling, that glass only feels more and more reinforced. We feel stuck between Good Friday and Easter Sunday — living, in a never ending Holy Saturday, witness to death and never tasting life.

4. Self-Hatred

"Good people would be better off without me."

Carol, a 25-year-old single woman, wrote this suicide note:

"Mom,
Jesus wants me. I want to be with Him.
Jesus told me I will be happy.
Job is also my friend. We talk much during the day.
I am His child.
Too much sins, too much evil!!"[12]

When people tell me I've done something wrong, I'm furious on the outside, but my soul repeats, "But it *is* your fault. Because everything is your fault." When I don't pay my rent on time. When I get a B. When someone is sad. When I look in the mirror. When I'm excluded by friends. When I'm rejected by a girl. When someone I know is suffering because of me. The suicidal heart absorbs those anxieties with a nod, one by one — "Yes, yes. You're a troublemaker. You should rid these good

---

[11] Dante Alighieri, *The Divine Comedy: Volume 1: Inferno*, Penguin Classics, trans. Mark Musa (New York: Penguin, 1984), 89.
[12] Ronald M. Holmes and Stephen T. Holmes, *Suicide: Theory, Practice, and Investigation* (Thousand Oaks, CA: Sage, 2005), 94.

people of your idiocy."[13] Yes, yes. Like a devilish "Our Father" prayer, my soul lisps suicidal scripts when the scene is right, hearing words from God given to me by a ventriloquist.

5. Resilience

> "Anyone who tells me not to kill myself
> simply doesn't understand."

Suicide digs its heels in, stubbornly insisting that needs are met. Speaking our own suicidal inclinations involves a hard balance. It's easy to think that if we listen to the need behind the pain, we give permission to commit suicide. But the opposite is true. Underneath despair lies grief. And deep within the kernel of grief there is a seed of release — catharsis. But where pain is critiqued, grief is denied. And where grief is denied, suicide speaks in its most soothing and hopeful voice: "End it. This person doesn't understand. No one will understand. It's because I'm right. There is no way for you to go on. It's okay."

Suicide tricks its victims into seeing survival as a spiritually selfish act, seeing survival as the source of anguish, seeing survival as the harrowing hallway of endless despair. The victim of suicidal ideations has had a pitchfork stuck through their imagination — unable to witness the good as good, the true as true, or the beautiful as beautiful. People who don't understand that speak with mute words.

God and Our Suicide

When suicide has received the understanding it wants, it stands with its chest out, proud and smiling. But it is at its weakest. God has so many beautiful weapons against suicide, as he fights for the lives of his

---

[13] Roy F. Baumeister argues that a common rationalization of suicide is "to create a state of cognitive construction . . . which helps prevent meaningful self-awareness and emotion. . . . making drastic measures seem acceptable." "Suicide As an Escape From Self," *Psychological Review* 97, no. 1 (1990): 90–113.

children.[14] Here are five.

1. Love

"God, help me to feel your love."

"You give yourself to us without judgment— after we have judged ourselves." God loves you. That falls flat. How can we experience God's love when our soul is tied to the operating table of suffering, the mad scientist? All we can do is gasp for air, like we've been kicked in the gut. And suicide calls most skillfully when we have run completely out of breath, even to breathe: "If I dwell in the remotest part of the sea, even there your hand will lead me" (Psalm 139:9). Just allow that verse five seconds. You dwell in the dark deep, where there is no light, no hope, no oxygen, just the suffocating pain of hopelessness. The Psalmist is with you: "Surely the darkness will hide me and the light become night around me." *It already has become unbearably dark.* Where does God show up?

Cut loose people who claim to speak for God, but only hurt you. Let them sink to the bottom of the sea, where you are. God isn't represented by them. He is in the moment with your mother, with your father, in the beginning: "For you created my inmost being; you knit me together in my mother's womb" (Psalm 139:13).

---

[14] It's very hard to find God in the fog of suicidality. Andrew Solomon, in his book *The Noonday Demon: An Atlas of Depression*, recounts a manic-depressive patient named Maggie, who had a conversation with her priest, that is a really helpful representation of the struggle people face: "According to Christian doctrine, you're not allowed to commit suicide, because your life is not your own. . . . You don't end up battling everything out inside yourself; you think you're battling it out with these other characters, with Jesus Christ and God the Father and the Holy Spirit. The Church is an exoskeleton for those whose endoskeleton has been eaten away by mental illness. You pour ourself into it and adapt to its shape." Maggie continues, "People think that Christianity is against pleasure, as it sometimes is; but it's very, very pro-joy. You're aiming for joy that will never go away, no matter what kind of pain you're in. But of course you still go through the pain. I asked my priest, when I wanted to kill myself, 'What's the purpose of this suffering?' and he said, 'I hate sentences that have the word *suffering* and the word *purpose* in them. Suffering is just suffering. But I do think that God is with you in this, though I doubt you can sense him at all.' I asked how I could put something like this in God's hands, and he said, 'There's no "put," Maggie. That's just where it is.'" *The Noonday Demon* (New York: Scribner, 2001), 132. Of course, God very well may have a purpose for your suffering. But he doesn't expect you to know it. And he doesn't expect the fact that there is a purpose to make it hurt less. Maybe that feeling of "battling Jesus" can dissolve a bit, when we realize that he is actually battling on our behalf, not against us (which is a very easy feeling to feel).

Think of your first moment on earth, and the happiness your mom and dad were filled with, as you came into the world. I'm not talking about all the pain that has transpired since then — all the broken relationships, the betrayal, the guilt, the death, the unbearable pain. In trying to remember this moment, we are scratched and clawed by our memories of abuse, and wrongdoing, and abandonment, and anger.

Cut past all of that. It's *had* its time controlling you. Just for a moment, find a glimpse of that first moment of your life — when you were celebrated with happiness; when your life and existence was an occasion for joy.

God created that moment. You were an occasion for God's joy. He cradles you, because he loves you so much. He loves you with the affection of a mother and a father, and better than our imperfect mothers and fathers who don't always know how to rejoice in us. God adores you. He created this whole universe, which is turned grey and depressing and unbearable for some of us, but he created it just to be with you. All of this stuff around you isn't loveless and impersonal. It certainly *feels* that way. "Even if it *is* personal, I can't feel it. I can't see it." It's *for* your joy. And the greatest lie we can believe is that it will be forever. God wants to cut the ropes that bind you to the anchor at the bottom of the ocean. The one who carefully watched over you from the day of your birth is with you at the bottom of the ocean now. And he is so desperately in love with you.

2. Self-Rudeness

"Screw off."

"I cry to you for help and you do not answer me;
    I stand, and you only look at me." (Job 30:20)

We have no energy for eloquent prayers! And no time. We have to do what we must: ... Fight. Cry. Kick. Scream. Punch. Bite. Scratch. Rip. Claw your way out. Grab the monster and put out his eyes.

"I'm throwing you a rope, you don't have to explain it to the monster in you, just tell the monster it can do whatever it wants, but not that. Later we'll get rid of the monster, for now just hanging on to the rope. I know that this means a struggle from one second to the next, let alone one day at a time."[15]

Stay. Stay here. Right now is not forever. Grief is so hard. It's so easy to believe you will always feel this way. Suffer here, with me. For some reason, I didn't kill myself. It wasn't rational. But I'm so happy I didn't. And on an unimaginable day, in the future, that is just as real as today, you will be happy. I can't tell you why or how. But you will.

If you hold on, you will suffer, but you will be happy again. Just stay here. There is hope here. Somebody will show up. Something will happen. Future you will be so happy you were brave, so thankful that you fought. This is your heroic moment. This is the fearful and painful moment — to keep walking when the monster has turned from a quiet suggester to a screaming accuser: "Do it! Do it! *DO IT!*"

The joy waiting for you on the other side of not giving up is immeasurable. It might be a month, a week, a day, a moment — but there is joy waiting for you. God understands your pain. He is with you, cheering you on, with a whole company of angels and saints throughout history, delighting in you and loving you as you overcome the impossible — as you *do* the impossible. "Therefore, since we are surrounded by so great a cloud of witnesses, let us also lay aside every weight, and sin which clings so closely, and let us run with endurance the race that is set before us" (Hebrews 12:1).

Do what you have to. Quit your job. Move back in with your parents. Delete your Facebook and social media accounts — and get off

---

[15] Hecht, *Stay*, xi.

the internet. Social media and internet use is linked with depression.[16] Once you have given suicide its due audience in understanding, spare no expense or effort in being doggedly rude with it. Like an audience who witnesses a boxer land a solid right hook, God loves seeing his children get scrappy and rude with their suicidal desires.

3. Solidarity

"You tried to kill yourself too? Why?"

When I was sitting on the edge of the Hudson River, crying, with my dad's gun, I called my college guidance counselor. Cliché, right? I don't know why I even had his number. I just knew I needed somebody who wasn't part of all my pain. I called him because I hadn't even seen him in four years. We were never friends. But I always had this sense about him that he was warm, and trustworthy, and a good man. So he answered, and stayed on the phone with me for six hours. And he told me to drive from New York to Philadelphia, to a counseling center. And I did. He stayed on the phone for the entire drive. And I met with someone.

---

[16] The medical field has coined the term "Facebook Depression" to refer to teenagers who stay online for so long that they start to exhibit symptoms of depression. And suicide is the number one cause of death among the depressed (Jouko K. Lönnqvist, "Psychiatric Aspects of Suicidal Behavior: Depression," in *The International Handbook of Suicide and Attempted Suicide*, ed. Keith Hawton and Kees van Heeringen (New York: Wiley & Sons, 2002), 117 [107–120].) With smart phones, are we ever *not* on the internet — thus, are we ever not at the mercy of crushing depression? Those "who suffer from Facebook depression are at risk for social isolation and sometimes turn to risky internet sites and blogs for 'help' that may promote substance abuse, unsafe sexual practices, or aggressive or self-destructive behaviors." (Glenn Schurgin O'Keefe, MD, Kathleen Clarke-Pearson, MD, and Council on Communications and Media, *Pediatrics* 127 (2011), 802 [800–804].) Do you feel bad? Science is finally saying: *unplug*. See also M.H.W. Selfhood, S.J.T. Brandi, M. Delsing, T.G.M. term Bogt, W.H.J. Em, "Different Types of Internet Use, Depression, and Social Anxiety: The Role of Perceived Friendship Quality," *Journal of Adolescence* 32, no. 4 (2009): 819–833; C. Huand, "Internet Use and Psychological Well-Being: A Meta-Analysis," *Cyberpsychology, Behavior and Social Networks* 13, no. 3 (2010): 241–249. See especially the work of Baylor business professor James Roberts, in James Roberts, Chris Pullig, and Chris Manolis, "I Need My Smartphone: A Hierarchical Model of Personality and Cell-Phone Addiction," *Personality and Individual Differences*, 79 (2015): 13–19. Depression, anxiety, and daytime dysfunction skyrockets among those who excessively use their smartphones: Kadir Demirci, Mehmet Agkönül, Abdullah Akpinar, "Relationship of Smartphone Use Severity with Sleep Quality, Depression, and Anxiety in University Students," *Journal of Behavioral Addictions* 4, no. 2 (2015): 85–92.

Call somebody trustworthy outside your circles.[17] Borrow money. And go to a counselor. You will see that you are not alone. They don't have to be Christian or orthodox or even the best. Just go to someone. Like a doctor with a broken leg, that counselor will know how to meet you in your pain and limp with you. You only have to fight long enough to collapse in the office of someone else. And when you're with them, don't hold back. Say everything you need to say. You're not alone. You want to kill yourself. But you don't want to die.

While suicide rates are scary, what's hopeful are treatment rates — 80–90% of people that seek treatment for depression are treated successfully using therapy and/or medication, even though 66% of depressed people don't seek help at all. Put yourself in that 90% is helped. God gives that kind of help in the right kind of church. The right friend will bring you to the right place.

4. Resolve

"No matter what, I'm not doing *that*."

Resolve to live. "Part of the recovery is to give up the suicide fantasies and threats and make a commitment to live, for better or worse. In essence, one has to close that back door, seal of the escape hatch, and get married to life with all its pain, paradox, and struggle."[18] Jesus has words for those teetering on the edge of suicide: "No, I tell you; but unless you repent, you will all likewise perish" (Luke 13:3). Don't think of that as a "judgmental" Christian rebuke. The Greek term for "repent" — *metanoia* — means "to turn your mind." It's not dismissive or inauthentic to push suicidal thoughts to a distance. If anything, suicidal thoughts are

---

[17] This can be awkward. In her book, Allie Brosh reflects on what it was like trying to tell a close friend that she was suicidal: "I didn't want it to be a big deal. However, it's an alarming subject. Trying to be nonchalant about it just makes it weird for everyone. I was also extremely ill-prepared for the position of comforting people. The things that seemed reassuring to me at the time weren't necessarily comforting for others: 'No, see, I don't necessarily want to KILL myself... I just want to become dead somehow. ssshhhhhhhhh... it's okay. Life is meaningless anyway. I'm really sorry. Can I get you some juice or something?'" Allie Brosh, *Hyperboly and a Half: Unfortunate Situations, Flawed Coping Mechanisms, Mayhem, and Other Things That Happened* (New York: Touchstone, 2013), 142–143.

[18] C. Karl, *Women, Sex, and Addiction* (New York: Harper and Row, 1989), 205.

invaders which seek to dismiss and destroy *your* true self.[19]

So, for the sake of free and open authenticity, repent — turn your mind — from these suicidal thoughts, turn from the path of those who perish, and look to Christ. Make up your mind to do so. Develop a plan to do so — plan to tell a friend you trust, or a person you trust, or throw away the gun, or run out of the house and go to the nearest trail and run until you know you're far enough away from tools of self-harm that you couldn't reach them easily. These are all things the Holy Spirit does. Do them, and you will see the Spirit on the move. There isn't any emotional meat here. Resolve is the skeleton of hope — lifeless, but sturdy and necessary.

5. Hope

> "This pain will pass.
> Even if it's been a really,

---

[19] Though not an enlisted soldiers, men may be caught in the internal turmoil and trauma of their war with themselves — between their own aspirations to honor and their corresponding lack of fruition. In the West, we often look at the Japanese act of staged self-death — *seppuku*, or *hari-kari* — as an unfortunate act of misinformed drama. "Why kill yourself over honor and shame?" we ask. "Just relinquish the ideology that makes those categories so weighty and choose a new belief system that doesn't require you to kill yourself." Yet, we would be ignorant to think that the mass male suicides in America today are not extensions of the same mythology. Self-staged death in Japan "became an important occasion for making a point of honor: a man's control, dignity, and concern for posthumous reputation all fused together with particular intensity at this point." (Eiko Ikegami, *The Taming of the Samurai: Honoring Individualism and the Making of Modern Japan* [Cambridge, MA: Harvard University Press, 1997], 103). Suicide as a product of bullying, especially, unveils this internal logic to our sensibilities: clawing for a sense of control, managing our reputations, reaching for the anchor of our dignity which we feel at times may only be uncoverable through grief over our own death. Have not these very preoccupations come to constitute our entire lives and emotions? Have they not driven us to into compulsive depths of dependence upon social media for affirmation and love — for public repute, i.e. honor? It is not inconceivable, then, how in a single season, failure to conform to arbitrary masculine-types (or feminine-types) could result in a morbid answer to what Albert Camus called the "one truly serious philosophical problem:" "Should I commit suicide?" The men of America have answered — non-soldiering men *stronger and better than us* have answered: "For honor, yes." Yet, Camus answers the question — he insists, that our very felt-existence (painful as it is) signifies our freedom to rebel against the call to self-kill. For Camus, it is not life, but the suicidal implication of life's perceived absurdity that challenges our will, against which we must exercise our passion, and our rebellion — this is our most profound and elemental act of humanity: to say "No" to suicide's tempting dare. When suicide's soothing voice whispers in our ear, it is not a voice to be avoided or ignored, but actively and deeply rebelled against: "I draw from the absurd three consequences, which are my rebellion, my freedom, and my passion. By the mere activity of consciousness, I transform into rule of life what was an invitation to death, and I refuse suicide." (Albert Camus, *The Myth of Sisyphus: And Other Essays* [New York: Alfred A. Knopf; Vintage, 1955, 1983], 62).

really long time."

Hope is the hardest part of moving away from suicide, because hopelessness is where it all began. Hopelessness is the ground zero of the suicide virus. And we may have a million reasons to accuse hope of abandoning us. "Many are saying of me, 'God will not deliver him'" (Psalm 3:2). Financial problems. Romantic heartbreak. Chronic depression. Helpless abandonment. Unkickable addiction. Emotional exhaustion. Some combination of it all. There will always be a reason to reject hope. But there will always be saints who defied those reasons: "I will not fear the tens of thousands drawn up against me on every side" (Psalm 3:6).

Every accusing voice, every echo of suicide's temptation, every hardship and heartbreak, they will come in and out of our lives like waves. Trying to *hope* in God in the midst of depression is like trying to breathe fresh air with your head dunked underwater. It's really, really, really hard. It feels like a sadistic world that we live in. But it is possible. To walk by faith is God's accomplishing the impossible through us, both when you hear birds chirping in the pines, and when you hear a screeching buzz at 60 decibels in the back of your head. High and low, God is still bringing a wave of joy your way, somehow. Hope. By surviving as long as you have, you have already earned the hero's title "_____, Doer of the Impossible."

Conclusion

You live a burdened life. But you are strong. And God is breathing strength into you right now — to hope, to take one more step, and then another. If you're alive, God is with you, hoping for you, walking with you, preparing people to help you. Make the phone call you need to make. If you have no one, call the National Suicide Prevention Lifeline: 1-800-273-8255.

The people there are actually really helpful. They're run by Ph.Ds in psychology. When I was in crisis, I thought this hotline was just a well-organized mob of well-meaning do-gooders who would yell at me: "Don'tdo it!" But I called them just to investigate for this chapter.

I'm really hard to counsel, because I'm stubborn and I usually think I'm smarter than my counselor. But these people really do know what they're doing. Call anyone. You don't have to call them. But it's not a bad idea. Think, "Who, in the past 10 years, could I call who could help me take one step in the right direction?" Make the call, one way or another. Future, happy you will be thankful you did.

> "I go about darkened, but not by the sun;
> I stand up in the assembly and cry for help."
> (Job 30:28)

Give someone a chance to advocate for truth on your behalf. You've let the monster have its day. Indeed, it's had its share of days, and relationships, and nights, and dollars, and happiness — consumed, like a black hole. Think about the story of Romeo and Juliet. Why is it a tragedy? Not because they each killed themselves — yes, that's tragic. But what makes it so painful is that they both *finally* had each other, but were so impatient with their tragedy that they killed themselves. If Romeo had only waited *a minute* before killing himself, life would have hinged, Juliet would have awoken, and they would have lived happily ever after.[20]

You don't know what the next minute will hold — the next month,

---

[20] Statistics show that if you could ask your post-suicide self "Do you regret it?" there is a 90% chance you would answer "Yes." *The Guardian* reported on a study of those who attempted to kill themselves: "Overwhelmingly, they regret it." (Melissa Davey, "Suicide Survival Stories Must Be Told, Says Australian Mental Health Chief," *The Guardian*, Wednesday July 23, 2014.
https://www.theguardian.com/society/2014/jul/24/suicide-survival-stories-must-be-told-says-australian-mental-health-chief. Accessed on July 25, 2016.) *The New Yorker* reported on those who survived suicide attempts by jumping off the Golden Gate bridge: "Survivors often regret their decision in midair, if not before." (Tad Friend, "Jumpers: The Fatal Grandeur of the Golden Gate Bridge," *The New Yorker*, October 13, 2003.
http://www.newyorker.com/magazine/2003/10/13/jumpers. Accessed on July 25, 2016) One medical journal surveyed over 90 studies on the statistics of suicide, and reported that 93% of those who attempt suicide never attempt again, indicating regret (while yet 40% of those who die from suicide have attempted previously — D. Owens, J. Horrocks, and A. House, "Fatal and Non-Fatal Repetition of Self-Harm: Systematic Review," *British Journal of Psychiatry* 181 [2002]: 193-199). This may be why more men kill themselves than women, even though women attempt suicide more: because their means are more lethal, more irrevocable, more concretely reinforced against the near-guaranteed regrets of their future selves (for more on this, see Matthew Miller and David Hemenway, "Guns and Suicide in the United States," *New England Journal of Medicine* 359 [2008]: 989-991).

or season. Don't let *one moment* of impatience with tragedy steal decades of happiness in front of you. They are there, for the taking, from the fatherly hand of God himself: "to accept his lot and rejoice in his toil—this is the gift of God" (Ecclesiastes 5:19). Stay here, with me — let's accept our lot, rejoice in our toil, and receive them both as gifts from God, awaiting a better day.

Appendix A:
Parenting Your Twentysomething Through Their Quarter Life Crisis

By Barbara Marrine (Paul's Mom)

There is no time like the present. In no other time in history has the cost of a college education has been so high, and the repayment of school loans such a burden. In no other time in history has addiction has been so prevalent, and so varied: to alcohol, illegal drugs, prescription drugs, sex and pornography — even addiction to work. In no other time in history has depression resulting in suicide has been so real a concern, lurking in the back of so many minds. Did I mention the breakdown of the family system? The modern family boasts of more divorce and dysfunction than our parents could have imagined in their lifetime. So, can we agree? There is no time like the present.

Our twentysomething "children" have been thrust (or thrust themselves) into a world that runs on change. There is new technology every month, with people waiting in line to get the newest upgrade. There are new modes of transportation: Do you have a Tesla yet? There are new careers: Have you met a molecular engineer (How about a social media architect)? There is a new social strata; what gender is your twentysomething? What about their friends?

What about their spouses!? Maybe you're really good at texting or tweeting, but if not (which is probably the case if you're over 50, like me), you may be closed out of a whole communication genre, limiting your ability to relate to (or stay in tune with) what is going on in your son/daughter's life. Change has never been so rapid as it is in the present.

The Challenges of Parenting a Twentysomething

In this time of unrivaled complexity, the task of parenting has become equally complicated. Here are five unexpected challenges that I faced when I became the parent of a twentysomething:

1. Giving Up Authority Over Them

How do you love your twentysomething in this decade/century? Loving a child is easy, concrete. You are relatively in control of every situation. You change their diaper, drive them to soccer practice, hold them and give them loving guidance when they are bullied at school, and teach them to drive. But loving a twentysomething is not as easy, not so concrete. We cannot so easily fix their pain. We cannot so quickly attend to their wounds. We cannot put them in time out, or threaten them with discipline. No, the world starts to do that for us. And as we relinquish our protective authority, and witness them step into the world's dangerous power on their own, it's very tempting to latch on to them in any way that we can. What else can we do with these instincts, twenty years in the making?

2. Witnessing Their New Life

Let's talk about the concept of control in the role of a parent. Whether you know it or not, your child is a "mini you," hence the word, "off-spring." Of course you want the best for your child — you know them better than anyone else in the world. You did change their diapers, after all! Well, as your child turns the corner into their third decade of life, you may not know them as well as you think. They have probably spent time away from home and the family dinner table. They have spent years in college, in military service, or just working relocated far away from their familiar upbringing. They probably have new friends, have traveled new places, and have developed their own opinions about life and the way things work. When they return, it can feel like the bond of love that has run on the bridge of familiarity for so long has been severed.

3. Letting Others Teach Them

There was a time when you were their only teacher. I remember my son coming home from kindergarten and showing me that he had learned to read. It was funny to me that he was learning from someone else now. I had taught him everything up to that point (Well, at least I thought I had). But now, as a twentysomething, the world has been their teacher. Your "off-spring" is not yours anymore. They are their own person, and it's your job to release control and take on a new role as the parent of an adult. We have been competent parents for so long. It's almost like training for a job in which we have no experience, learning the skill of parenting a twentysomething does not come natural to many of us. Now we have to learn to let our twentysomethings learn from others.

4. Watching Them Fail

What does it mean to become the parent of an adult? Do we need a new category? Or is the relationship something like a good old friend, or a colleague that you work with — or does it fit in the niece/nephew category? I'm here to tell you that being the parent of an adult is its own category. Yes, they are their own person, but they still consider you as a parent. As this generation enters their twentysomethings, they face the fast-paced we've already mentioned, but also a slowing-down of the transition into adulthood. Many of them are having difficulty finding a career position, making enough money (or having too many school loans) to purchase their own home, and waiting to marry and have children.

The time of life when *we found ourselves* making all our first "adult" decisions has been elongated for them. All the stresses of finding a job, deciding where to live, falling in love and deciding to marry, are happening over a period of ten to fifteen years instead of two to five years. This leads to a extended time of uncertainty for our twenty-something's and this uncertainty for them. This usually implies an uncertainty for us, as parents. This is very hard for us to watch, because it's so easy to think about the new experience of twentysomethings as a failure through our own experience, twenty or thirty years removed. (We also are sometimes the ones who have to *foot the bill* for the failure). Watching our children strike out on their own isn't easy. We want to step out onto the field and give them ice cream, but we aren't right in the stands anymore. They're in Chicago, or Los Angeles, or New York, or Philadelphia. It's not easy watching somebody we love so deeply hurt from afar.

5. Witnessing Their Uncertainty

Uncertainty can conjure up so many emotions: impatience, anxiety, frustration and even anger. Due to our own experience, which differs from that of our twenty-something's, we have difficulty understanding what they are going through. This is often exacerbated by the fact that some of their responsibilities and/or needs may fall on us now. They may be moving back home after college, possibly without a job or career goal. Paying college loans may be an issue. There might be a need of treatment for addiction or emotional distress, and possibly be in denial. Can you relate? One of my favorite lines to say when my son is having a difficult time is, "Just breathe." And yes, there is no time like the present.

You might be ready to put this book down and say, "So far all I'm reading is doom and gloom!" Maybe your twentysomething is doing just fine — employed, content with their living arrangements, engaged or married, and downright happy with life. If so, congratulations! But I think the next five bullet points will be helpful, because as you know, life does not go on happily for decades at a time.

God and Our Parenting

As we examine life with our twenty-something, I suggest we consider the blessing God has bestowed upon us, and a challenge for us to understand how we can bring glory to God in this opportunity as a parent of a twentysomething adult. God has cared for more twentysomethings than we ever have. He was the one who cared for *us* in our twenties. Here are five ways that we can participate in God's care for our twentysomething children:

1. Be Thankful

> "Adam made love to his wife Eve, and she became pregnant and gave birth to Cain. She said, 'With the help of the LORD I have brought forth a man.'"
> (Gen. 4:1)

Let us remember that our parenthood is a gift from God. He has blessed us with children and entrusted them to our care. When I think about my children, I am at a loss for words to express the extent of my love for them. The blessing of parenthood is multiplied by the delight and awe experienced as the years go by. I know my words are bringing your own appreciation for parenthood to mind right now.

I am an educator, and in the past few years, have learned about a strategy called *responsive writing*. This might prove to be a good technique for you to reflect on the blessing God has granted to you, as a parent of your twentysomething. I suggest you simply make a list of all that you love about your son/daughter. Another topic to reflect on is the special memories you hold dear. Keep this list of blessings close by to reference on a regular basis. There is no time like the present to focus on all that you admire in your twentysomething, and reflect on the wonderful things that God is doing — the big, and the little things — in gratitude for God's blessing of parenthood.

2. Surrender

> And when she had weaned him, she took him up with her, along
> with a three-year-old bull, an ephah of flour, and a skin of wine,
> and she brought him to the house of the LORD at Shiloh. And
> the child was young. Then they slaughtered the bull, and they
> brought the child to Eli. And she said, "Oh, my lord! As you live,
> my lord, I am the woman who was standing here in your
> presence, praying to the LORD. For this child I prayed, and the
> LORD has granted me my petition that I made to him.
> Therefore I have lent him to the LORD. As long as he lives, he
> is lent to the LORD." And he worshiped the LORD there.
> (1 Samuel 1:24-28 ESV)

Do you remember the story of Hannah? She prayed for a child
and in her prayer, she said that she would give the child to the Lord. So
after he was weaned, she gave her son, Eli, to the Priest, Samuel. Talk
about surrender! Actually, yes, let's talk about surrender. It's important
to note: it's not enough to say, "children are a blessing." God has blessed
us with our children. They are from God. Hannah said, "For his whole
life he will be given over to the Lord." Even when he is a
twentysomething.

Of course, it is most difficult to surrender when you're
twentysomething is having difficulty. That's when you want to help.

You want to fix their situation. If only you could save them from
going through the same pain you faced as a young adult. You try to give
them advice. You slip into "suggestion mode," brainstorming possible
solutions to the problem. You say, "I could help you with your resume!"
or "Maybe she's not the right girl for you." Or the traditional, "Do you
really *need that?*"

But, it never goes well, because they are not children any more.
Your twentysomething is an adult, and most probably, you have given
them all this advice before. They know how to apply for a job and find
the right girl and how to budget their money. They know all that you
have to offer, because you have told them many times before. The only
thing that stands between your suggestions and success is experience.
And you cannot give them that! They will make mistakes. And they may
even make many of *your* mistakes. That doesn't make you a failure as a

parent. If anything, their mistakes will be both their opportunity to mature in their skill *and* their trust in a God who grows imperfect people into less imperfect people. So, there is no time like the present to surrender your twentysomething to life and to God.

3. Study

As my son, Paul, entered his twentysomething years, he was dealing with depression. He was living about 4 hours away, so I could not spend face-to-face time with him. However, we talked on the phone a great deal. Some of our conversations went well, but most of the time he was frustrated with what I had to say. I wanted so much to help, but my words (focused on solutions) were not helpful. It wasn't until I read, *Where Is God When it Hurts?*, by Philip Yancy that I learned to just be there for him.[1]

I learned that just to say, "I love you" and "I am here for you" was enough to help him remember that someone cared for him. Just acknowledging that I was hearing what he was saying brought him some comfort. I learned that it was better to allow him to be depressed instead of trying to talk him out of how he was truly feeling. Fortunately, Paul was working with a professional Christian counselor who provide the necessary assistance he needed.

Our twentysomethings face many challenges in this day and age. Letting them know that you are there for them, in your words and deeds, is essential to harvesting a supportive relationship. They need you in their lives. Learning all you can about their issues, whatever it might be — depression, addiction, financial challenges — will make all the difference. Take time to read, research, and speak to professionals. Also remember to rely on your pastor, wise Biblical counsel, and prayer as you make decisions and interact with your son/daughter. We're not trying to *fix* their issues like we once could when they were small. But we are trying to be *with* them by understanding them. To that end, there is no time like the present to study.

---

[1] Philip Yancey, *Where Is God When It Hurts?* (Grand Rapids, MI: Zondervan, 2002).

4. Listen

"My sheep listen to my voice; I know them, and they follow me." (John 10:27)

When we read John 10:27, we have a deep understanding of what it is to really listen, and to really know someone. As parents, we have probably not spent a lot of time listening to our children. For so long, our role was more about telling them what they need to know or what they need to do. We wanted them to follow us. Well, the tide has turned. It is now time, more than ever, to listen to what our twentysomething is saying. Listening enables us to know who they are. It gives us information about their world, which we are unfortunately not always part of.

There is a scene from the musical-film *West Side Story* where the young gang Jets are fighting with the other gang, Sharks. The cops try to intervene. One cop says to one of the gang members, "When I was your age... " and the Jet interrupts, "When *you* was my age? When my old man was my age, when my brother was my age ... You was never my age, none of ya! And the sooner you creeps get hip to that, the sooner you'll dig us!" Listening is our ticket into the event — the event of their lives and the event of our relationship with them. What is it like to be a twentysomething *today*? In twenty, thirty years, they'll need to do a lot more listening. But today, we ask, "How are you, really?"

But listening is more than information gathering. When you are really listening, you are letting them know how much you care about them. Listening is a direct act of love. Uninterrupted listening is the best. It can be over coffee or a meal. It could be during a walk or long car ride. It could be over a text message or email or maybe you are good enough with your technology to FaceTime.

A friend of mine was having a "dispute" over text message with his twentysomething son. When they got to a heated climax, my friend texted, "We need to talk!" His son texted back, "About what?" My friend asked for advice about how to handle the dispute. After some thought, I suggested that he continue texting with his son to allow for more comfortable communication for his son. However you do it, there is no time like the present to listen.

5. Love

"Be completely humble and gentle;
be patient, bearing with one another in love."
(Ephesians 4:2)

I was once visiting Paul after not seeing him for several months. We went to dinner and grabbed a few things at the grocery store. Upon returning to his apartment, we sat down to watch a show on TV, when he reached over to hug me and started sobbing. Paul has always been an intense kind of guy. I shouldn't have been surprised that he had been feeling lonely and sad for some time. But I was taken off guard by his intense sobbing. We hugged and he cried for a few minutes. After some time to talk (with me listening to the best of my ability) Paul regained his composure and the night went on. These moments showed me just how much pain our twentysomethings hold inside. I was so glad that he was able to let out his feelings with me. There is no time like the present to love our twentysomething children.

Conclusion

We do need to be gentle and patient, bearing all these ups and downs with all our love for twentysomethings. This is where we do remain parents. Sometimes we are the only place in their life where they can let go. Love is the covering for all the disciplines mentioned. Being grateful for the gift of life that God has entrusted to our care, while at the same time surrendering who they are and what they will become, keeping abreast of contemporary issues through study and listening to know and as an act of care lie under the umbrella of love. It is God's gift of love given through the Holy Spirit that allows us to accomplish all that is required to parent a twenty-something. I urge you to pray for the Holy Spirit to fill you with love and fruit as you parent your wonderful twenty-something.

Appendix B:
Discussion Questions

Chapter 1
Quarter Life Crisis

Read this Bible verse before reading the discussion questions aloud:

> "Let each person lead the life
> that the Lord has assigned to him,
> and to which God has called him"
> (1 Corinthians 7:17).

Discussion Questions

- The quarter life crisis is defined here as "a season when we realize: we are promised no earthly thing in this life." If you feel like you're in the midst of your own quarter life crisis, what event caused this realization?

- Does the definition of quarter life crisis resonate with you, or does it fall a bit short of your experience?

- How would your personal experience lead you to define the term "quarter life crisis" differently?

- Which promises of God (if any) feel as steady as the first day you became a Christian, and which promises (if any) feel much less uncertain?

Chapter 2
Depression

Read this Bible verse aloud before reading the discussion questions aloud:

> Though the fig tree does not blossom,
>   and no fruit is on the vines;
> ...
> *yet* I will rejoice in the LORD;
>   I will exult in the God of my salvation."
>   (Habakkuk 3:17–18)

Discussion Questions

- We usually associate *sadness* with depression. What "symptom" do you most commonly associate with depression?

- While there is an entire appendix devoted to the issue of medication, what has your personal experience been with medication? Those you know who take medication for depression — how long have they used the medication, and has it helped them to develop a fuller life, and do they continue to exhibit symptoms of depression? (This is not a loaded question — be as objective and descriptive as possible; avoid explanation)

- Does the command "Rejoice in the Lord always; again, I will say, rejoice!" (Phil. 4:4) feel like a liberation or a burden (or a mixture of both)?

- The conclusion of the chapter defines joy as a "skill." What are the limits of that metaphor? Is it appropriate to consider moments of deep depression as similar to "stumbling" during practice while learning the skill of joy — like falling while learning a handstand, or hitting the wrong note on a piano scale?

Chapter 3
Loneliness

Read this Bible verse aloud before reading the discussion questions aloud:

"Turn to me and be gracious to me,
  for I am lonely and afflicted."
      (Psalm 25:16)

Discussion Questions

- If intimacy is scary for you, what is the thing that scares you most about being known? If it is hard, what is the hardest thing?

- Do you have a standard to which you hold others? In other words, do you often find yourself getting angry at others for the way they act with you, their habits of relating to you? Does that help you "sift out" unsafe people, or hinder your intimacy with others (or both)?

- When is the last time that God's presence in your life, in your very space, was meaningful to you? What made it meaningful?

- What are positive and negative ways that the church intersects with loneliness? Does it ever make you feel more lonely, or less?

Chapter 4
Lust

Read this Bible verse aloud before reading the discussion questions aloud:

> "Go, show your love to your wife again, though she is loved by another and is an adulteress. Love her as the LORD loves the Israelites, though they turn to other gods and love the sacred raisin cakes."
> (Hosea 3:1).

Discussion Questions

- We are often caught between the longing to be loved produced by our abstinence, and our regret from pursuing love in the wrong way. Which feeling — longing or regret — feels worse?
- If you had total domain over your sexual activity as a single person, what would your life look like?
- What would a perfect sexual relationship look like in a marriage? What priority would it have in the relationship? How often would it occur? What would that experience *do* for you? For your spouse? For God?
- Do you ever feel like God's moral requirements about sexuality are too difficult to obey? If so, when is it easiest, and when is it hardest?

Chapter 5
Anxiety

Read this Bible verse aloud before reading the discussion questions aloud:

> "Say to those who have an anxious heart, 'Be strong; fear not! Behold, your God will come with vengeance, with the recompense of God. He will come and save you.'"
> (Isaiah 35:4).

Discussion Questions

- When you get anxious, is there a common "trigger" — a person, a place, an event, a sound, a smell, a concept? If so, what does that "trigger" threaten?

- How does God relate differently to our good fears (for example, the desire to protect those we love), and our overwhelming fears (for example, or desire to protect our family which borders on paranoia)?

- Let's call Philippians 4:6 Paul, "Courageous Paul" ("do not be anxious about anything"), and Philippians 2:28 Paul, "Concerned Paul" (who wants to see his friends "that I may be less anxious"). Courage and Concern are both loving virtues. Which "Paul" do you find more helpful for overcoming your own fears? Is it more helpful to hear that your fears are legitimate concerns (Phil. 2:28), or that God calls us to trust him when we feel anxious (Phil. 4:6)?

Chapter 6
Dissatisfaction

Read this Bible verse aloud before reading the discussion questions aloud:

> "So teach us to number our days
>   that we may get a heart of wisdom.
> Return, O LORD! How long?
>   Have pity on your servants!
> Satisfy us in the morning with your steadfast love,
>   that we may rejoice and be glad all our days."
>   (Psalm 90:12-14)

Discussion Questions

- What are your unspoken expectations for this upcoming year? Five years? Ten years?

- When is the last time you remember being satisfied with you life? What were the major circumstantial differences between that time and now?

- Pray to God this honest prayer: "I *need* (_____), and you're wrong/bad/unloving if you withhold it from me." What is the (_____)?

- When is the last time you remembered being satisfied with God? What were the major differences between who you were then and who you are now?

Chapter 7
Self-Hatred

Read this Bible verse aloud before reading the discussion questions aloud:

> "I have no greater joy than to hear that
> my children are walking in the truth."
> (3 John 1:4).

Discussion Questions

- Usually one "thing" will spin us into self-hatred consistently: a past mistake, an ex-girlfriend/boyfriend, a failure, a regret. What spins you into self-hatred?

- Self-hatred is often the product of a lying, serious voice. What are contexts that make it easy for you to "unwind" or "relax your shoulders?" What people, or places, or songs, or feelings make it easy for you to laugh at the absurdity of your negative circumstances?

- When was the last time you believed a positive thing someone said to you — and didn't write it off as pity?

- Do you often believe that God wants you to hate yourself? How would it change the way you wake up in the morning if you knew that God wanted to bless you with the joy of self-love today?

Chapter 8
Doubt

Read this Bible verse aloud before reading the discussion questions aloud:
"Now I want to remind you, although you once fully knew it, that Jesus, who saved a people out of the land of Egypt, afterward destroyed those who did not believe. . . . But you, beloved, building yourselves up in your most holy faith and praying in the Holy Spirit, keep yourselves in the love of God, waiting for the mercy of our Lord Jesus Christ that leads to eternal life. And have mercy on those who doubt."
(Jude 1:5, 20-22)

Discussion Questions

- If you were to put all your cards on the table, what are you scared is the one silver bullet question that could destroy your faith in that Jesus Christ loves you, is good to you, and cares about you? Is it an atheistic argument, or the reliability of Scripture, the question of evolution — or is it an event, like the death of a loved one?

- It is very hard to detach our experience of God from our experience of the people who introduced us and taught us to him. Does it help our suspicions about God to distinguish between God *as he has been presented to us* and God *as he is, for us, with us, distinct and distant from the people who hurt us?* If not, ask yourself this question instead: What does God think about the fact that you were hurt by his people?

- Has your lingering doubt helped you to become a happier person, or has it distanced you from your "self"?

- If Scripture has one word about God's attitude toward *doubters*, it is "mercy" (Luke 18:13; Jude 1:22). What do you often feel is God's attitude toward you? Is it "Indifference"? Or malice? Or carelessness? Or heavyhandedness? Or sternness? Or incompetence? What does it mean that "mercy" is the opposite of all of those words?

Chapter 9
Grief

Read this Bible verse aloud before reading the discussion questions aloud:

> "But we do not want you to be uninformed, brothers, about those who are
> asleep, that you may not grieve as others do who have no hope."
> (1 Thessalonians 4:13)

Discussion Questions

- What loss has been most devastating for you in the past 5 years? 10 years? Why?

- Not everyone grieves the same way. Some people move on very quickly. Others are deeply impacted forever. What feeling did you have about your loss — romantic, parental, or biographical? Was it despair — "Will I feel this sad forever?" Sadness — "I wish I could see them one more time." Anger — "This isn't fair." Numbness — "I can't afford to 'deal' with this right now." Or something else?

- When God raises us all from the dead, he won't "white wash" our identities and earthly lives, but bring us back to them in their most glorious and beautiful moments. Does that reality feel harsh or soothing?

- In those grey, lonely moments of sadness, God is the one who cherishes old trinkets, and little memories, and nostalgic feelings. What memory about the thing you've lost do you think God cherishes most?

Chapter 10
Regret

Read this Bible verse aloud before reading the discussion questions aloud:

> "Godly grief produces a repentance
> that leads to salvation without regret,
> whereas worldly grief produces death."
> (2 Corinthians 7:8-10)

Discussion Questions

- What regretful decision came to mind as you read this chapter? Was it *sinful*, or was it merely painful?

- Who is the one person at the center of your regret? It may be a parent, a spouse, an ex, a friend, even yourself or God.

- How does it land on you — the notion that God, who is omniscient and omnipresent and perfectly wise — chooses to experience the regret of negative consequences for good decisions, because he finds it a worthy cost to be with us?

Chapter 11
Suicidality

Read this Bible verse aloud before reading the discussion questions aloud:

> "I will not fear the tens of thousands
> drawn up against me on every side."
> (Psalm 3:6)

Discussion Questions

- What hypothetical situation would "fix" your feeling? It can be absurd. What would it be? Someone coming back from the dead? Your reputation restored? A relationship reconciled? Imagine your dream world, that would fix it all. What would that *thing* be that would dissolve your desire to kill yourself?

- How would you feel if God told you that *that life* you mentioned will exist for you — or a comparable form of it — in 20 years? Would you wait, or would you kill yourself? What if it was 10 years? What about 5? If it was 5 years out guaranteed, what would you do for the next 5 years?

- How does it change your perspective on suicide to know that suicide is the third highest cause of death among twentysomethings? What about the fact that of those who seek help (through counseling or medication), over 90% report drastic improvement of emotional wellbeing?

- God has something better for you than suicide. He had something better for me than suicide. Not immediately. But the heroic resilience that you've already shown so far can one day blossom into a life of joy. Will you stay here, on earth, with me?

Appendix A
Parenting Your Twentysomething Through Their Quarter Life Crisis

Read this Bible verse aloud before reading the discussion questions aloud:

> "So if there is any encouragement in Christ . . . Do nothing from selfish ambition or conceit, but in humility count others more significant than yourselves."
> (Philippians 2:1, 3)

Discussion Questions

- What are you thankful for about your twenty something?
- Think of your last conversation with your twentysomething. Did you listen to them? What did they really say?
- What do you wish your twentysomething understood about you?
- What do you need to surrender control of?
- What does loving your twentysomething look like? Feel like?
- Where are your triggers (events, words, feelings, moments) that cause you to become anxious, angry, or sad?

Made in the USA
Middletown, DE
11 May 2018